Cut College Costs

How to

Get Your Degree –
Without Drowning in Debt

Rose Rennekamp

Cut College Costs

How to Get Your Degree – Without Drowning in Debt

Rose Rennekamp

Books> Education> Higher Education> Financial Aid

Books> Education> Higher Education> College Guides

ISBN-13: 978-1499716290

ISBN-10: 149971629X

Library of Congress Control Number: 2014919239

CreateSpace Independent Publishing Platform,
North Charleston, SC

Disclaimer: The author has made every attempt to ensure the accuracy of information presented in this book. However, there are bound to be changes between the time information is collected and an individual reads this book. The author recommends readers do their own in-depth research before making decisions about subjects discussed in this book.

ABOUT THE AUTHOR

One of Rose Rennekamp's life goals is to help open doors of opportunity through education. She was the first in her family to earn a baccalaureate degree, and she is grateful for the opportunities it gave her.

Rose has counseled students in middle school through graduate school, and has written widely about college and career planning. More than 250 newspapers across the country carried her column, *College and Career Corner*, written while she was vice president of communications at ACT, Inc.

Her writing will never win literary awards. And it isn't lighthearted or entertaining. The goal of her writing is simple: to provide accurate information that is easy to understand. She writes college and career information at an eighth grade reading level. The advice she provides is practical and easy to implement.

Rose has undergraduate and graduate degrees in education, counseling, and marketing. She has taught undergraduate and graduate courses at the University of Iowa. She is board president of the Iowa College Access Network and a board member of the Kirkwood Community College Foundation.

ACKNOWLEDGMENTS

Thank you

...to my parents and grandparents for making learning a high priority,

...to my children who inspired me to write this book,

...to my husband who encouraged me to keep writing,

...and to the E.T. Meredith Foundation, that provided the scholarship that allowed me to go to college.

Table of Contents

INTRODUCTION

If you're like most people, you're convinced college is important for success. But you're concerned about cost. And it seems less affordable every day.

Increases in tuition and fees have outpaced inflation for many years. Financial aid hasn't kept pace. And family savings and income have grown more slowly than college prices.

If you've saved for college thinking prices would increase at the rate of inflation, you're in for a big surprise. According to the College Board, the average published price for tuition, fees, room, and board at a US private non-profit college in 2014 - 2015 was more than $42,000 – for one year. Even at state universities, the published price for in-state students was nearly $19,000 per year. And the average tab at a community college was more than $11,000.

Students must also pay for books, supplies, laundry, transportation, and entertainment. And most students don't complete a two-year degree in two years or a four-year degree in four.

Thank goodness for financial aid! But state and federal aid haven't increased as fast as tuition and fees. Plus, there are fewer grants (that you don't have to pay back) and more loans (that you do have to pay back). Also, limits on federal subsidized loans haven't kept up with college prices. So, people have to borrow at higher interest rates.

According to the Project on Student Debt, about seven in ten college students now graduate with student loan debt. The average debt at graduation is more than $28,000. That doesn't include credit card debt, or parent debt. Nearly four in ten full-time students graduate with unmanageable levels of debt according to the Public Interest Research Group's (PIRG) Higher Education Project. PIRG defines unmanageable debt as federal loan payments that are more than 8 percent of a graduate's income.

The difficult economy of these past several years hit families hard. Many families' income and **net worth** (what they own, minus what they owe) have declined. Plus, graduates are facing weak job markets. And people who get jobs often don't earn the salaries they expect. So, many students and families are rethinking how much they're willing to borrow for college.

Several studies show graduates are surprised at the size of their student loan payments. Many turn down jobs they want and accept better-paying employment to pay off loans. And many aren't paying, so their debt keeps growing.

Sounds dismal, doesn't it? But while the good news is scarce, you *can* afford college. This book will show you how. Many upper-middle-income families don't qualify for need-based financial aid. And many students who are "college material" simply aren't good enough in academics, athletics, music, or drama to get scholarships. But whether you qualify for financial aid or not, this book can help you save thousands off the price of college.

This book won't give you step-by-step instructions. There are hundreds of ways to save on college costs. No tactic is right for every student. And some don't work if you use others. There is no one correct path for all students – or even one correct approach for a single student.

This book has five parts. Part One (Chapters 1-2) helps you learn the language, so you'll understand what you're reading. Skim these chapters. Then refer to them later, if needed. Part Two (Chapters 3-8) will help you get ready for college. Part Three (Chapters 9-22) outlines paths you could take to get your degree. Part Four (Chapters 23-28) deals with narrowing the choices, applying to colleges, and deciding where to enroll. Part Five (Chapters 29-45) is about saving money while you're in college.

How should you read this book? Of course, you can read it cover to cover. I've tried to arrange chapters in a logical order. But each chapter stands alone. So, you can read just the chapters you want. If you already know the terms used to describe college and financial aid, you can skip Chapters 1 and 2. If you would never go to school outside the US, skip Chapter 18. If you know you'll never enter the military, skip Chapter 19, too. Focus on chapters that are most meaningful for you.

Some people will read this book as part of a college prep class, with conversations after each chapter. It's a great way to think through ideas with other people. Parents may also want to read with their teens. Maybe you could read a few chapters each weekend, and then talk about them during the week. Or perhaps a friend is thinking about college. If so, make plans to read a few chapters. Then get together and discuss them.

Take notes as you read. Write down ideas that sound interesting. Then you might want to reread a chapter or two. Or you might read this book before high school, and then reread it after a couple of years to help plan your next steps.

Try to read with an open mind. Don't reject ideas until you know enough to say, "That's not for me." Try to keep your mind open throughout college. Ideas that don't sound good when you're 18 might look great when you're 21!

Use tools beyond this book. For example, this book doesn't give details about individual colleges. You'll want to get the latest information from their websites. This book also doesn't provide details about selecting the right college. There are many good, free, online services that'll help you match schools to your needs.

I've included **URLs** (online addresses for websites). They were all correct and active when I published the book. But we all know that websites come and go, and some change addresses. I apologize if you're unable to connect with one.

Try not to become anxious as you read. If you do, stop and take a break. As I was writing, I worried that I might be including too much information. I worried that readers might become confused. There is a lot to understand! If I've confused you, or caused you to be anxious, I apologize. My goal is to give you accurate information that you can think about in manageable chunks. So again, if you become confused or anxious, take a break and come back later.

As you read this book, you'll find no "right" answers. This book merely shows you alternatives. You have to figure out what makes sense for you.

Seneca, a first century Roman philosopher, said, "Luck is what happens when preparation meets opportunity." This book will help you understand opportunities. It will also help you prepare to take advantage of them. Good luck!

CHAPTER 1 – UNDERSTAND THE LANGUAGE OF COLLEGE

So, you want to go to college. Fantastic! There are thousands of colleges in the United States. Even if you have family responsibilities and need to stay close, you'll have many choices.

This chapter outlines the types of colleges. It defines many of the special words associated with college, too. The definitions are US definitions. They sometimes have different meanings outside the US, even in English language countries. You may not have heard many of the terms before. And frankly, the definitions are changing and blurring.

High school counselors, college admissions officers, scholarship committees, and financial aid professionals use special terms when they talk about college. So, you'll want to understand them. I've defined key college terms the first time they appear in this book. The terms are in **boldface type**. Don't try to memorize definitions. (There won't be a test. I promise!) Just read the definitions to get an idea of what words mean. You can always refer back to these sections later, if needed.

The terms **postsecondary education** and **higher education** describe education past high school. Some people use the word **college** to describe any education beyond high school where you can earn a credential. A **credential** confirms something. Students can earn several types of credentials, including degrees, certificates, certifications, badges, and licenses.

Most people have a narrower definition of **college**. They use it to describe any school that awards associate or bachelor's degrees. Most colleges and universities award one or the other, but not both. A **university** is a family of colleges that also offers advanced degrees. A person "going to college" could be going to a two-year school, a small four-year school, or a very large university. This book uses the word "college" in this way. I use "college" and "schools" when talking about education institutions that offer associate or bachelor's degrees. If I'm referring to just one type of college, I try to say that.

Colleges award credentials to students who complete precise requirements. For example, you can earn a **degree** after you complete specific requirements. The requirements depend on the degree and **major** (field of study). Some schools use the term **concentration** rather than major. To earn a degree with a particular major or concentration, students must complete (and earn passing grades in) a set of required classes. Students **declare** (decide) their majors at different times, depending on the college. At some schools, students declare a meta-major early, and then declare their major later. A **meta-major** is a broad subject area. For example, you might declare business as a meta-major. You'd then take classes that would apply to several different business majors. You'd then declare your major (accounting, finance, marketing, human resources, etc.) later on. A college has **departments**. Departments can include several majors (programs of study).

Schools often have strict guidelines about titles, contents, and books for **required classes**. Most classes have letter grades (A, B, C, D, or F). Most degrees also include **elective classes** (sometimes called **electives**). There are fewer guidelines for electives, so students have more choices. Students must still earn passing grades in electives. Some electives have only Pass or Fail grades. To earn a degree, you must also sometimes pass exams, do research, write a paper, or complete a large project. If you complete the requirements of two majors, you can get a **double major**. Some schools award a **minor** if you complete a shorter series of classes in a subject. You **graduate** after you earn your degree. When you graduate, you receive a **diploma** (certificate). The graduation event is **commencement**.

A **prerequisite** is something that must occur before something else can happen. For example, you sometimes have to take one class before you can take another. Or you might need to be at least 21 to take a class about wine.

At most schools, students complete a set number of **credit hours** (sometimes just called **credits**) to earn a degree. Credit hours normally are determined by the time you're in class and need to study outside class. Students who get passing grades all get the same credits for a class. In **competency-based education**, students earn credit when they prove they have specific skills, abilities, and knowledge in a subject.

People often describe degrees by the number of years needed to complete the degree (for example, two-year, and four-year). However, many students go to school only part time and they sometimes switch majors. So, most students don't graduate within these periods. Most students take longer than two years to get a two-year degree. And most students take longer than four years to get a four-year degree.

Community colleges (sometimes called **two-year colleges**, **freshman-sophomore campuses**, or **associate colleges**) are public schools. Most students at a community college are from the local area, and many stay in the area after graduation. Community colleges award **associate degrees** (though some community colleges now offer bachelor's degrees, too). An associate degree usually requires about sixty credits. The degree is usually an Associate of Arts (A.A.) or Associate of Science (A.S.), depending on the major. Some community college job training programs lead to an Associate of Applied Science (A.A.S.) degree. An A.A.S. is a **terminal degree**. This means that credits usually can't count toward another degree. Some people use the term **academic degree** to describe those that can count toward a further degree and the term occupational degree to describe those that can't. An **occupational degree** is one "for which the primary purpose is gainful employment and career development," according to the Accrediting Council for Continuing Education and Training.

Community colleges also offer job training. **Job training programs** often take less than two years to complete. They prepare students to enter the workforce. They often include **apprenticeships.** Apprenticeships offer experiential learning. **Experiential learning** uses real-world situations to develop your knowledge and skills. Apprenticeships are "learn and earn" programs. You work, earn money, and learn from experts on the job. Electricians, plumbers, ironworkers, and other tradespeople train through apprenticeships. There are also nursing, information technology, truck driving, and advanced manufacturing apprenticeships. Apprenticeship programs usually lead to certificates, licenses, or certifications rather than associate degrees.

A **certificate** shows you have completed a set of requirements. The requirements can include courses, exams, and other tasks. Schools (and other trainers) award certificates. Some certificates are only **certificates of attendance**. They prove you were there, not that you learned anything. Certificates of attendance aren't valuable when you look for a job. Employers want proof you have skills.

A **certification** shows you have the abilities, skills, and knowledge to perform a job. Students complete written, oral, or performance-based exams to display skills, knowledge, and abilities. Independent organizations (other than schools and government agencies) award certifications. In some job-focused training, you can earn **industry endorsements** or **badges**. These certifications show you have the skills to do specific tasks. Some people call these **stackable credentials**. When you learn new job skills, you can earn more endorsements or badges. These may help you get higher-level, better-paying jobs.

Government agencies award licenses. For example, you may have a driver's license issued by the state where you live.

A **license** is a permit to own or do something. Electricians, plumbers, doctors, dentists, cosmetologists, and funeral directors must all have licenses. Their licenses allow them to perform a specific occupation in a defined geographic area. Requirements for a license can include a college degree, certifications, certificates, exams, apprenticeships, or work experience. People who hold licenses must periodically renew them.

Community colleges also offer **general interest** and **continuing education courses**. For example, a community college might offer courses in personal finance, cooking, poetry, and home maintenance. These courses provide no academic credit. They don't count toward degree or certificate requirements.

Community colleges usually have open admissions. **Open admissions** (sometimes called **open enrollment** or **open access**) means that anyone who graduated high school can enroll. People who have a **GED (General Educational Development)** or **High School Equivalency Test (HiSET)** can also enroll. The GED and HiSET are alternatives to a high school diploma. Even if a college has open admissions, some programs may have stricter requirements.

Undergraduate, **bachelor's degree**, or **baccalaureate colleges** (often called **four-year colleges**) offer a wide variety of courses and programs. (People often say **undergrad** rather than undergraduate.) These schools award **baccalaureate** (or **bachelor's**) **degrees**. Bachelor's degrees can be one of several kinds. For example, a school may offer Bachelor of Arts (B.A.), Bachelor of Science (B.S.), Bachelor of Fine Arts (B.F.A.) or Bachelor of Business Administration (B.B.A.) degrees. Students need about 120 credits for most bachelor's degrees.

Students earn **graduate degrees** (or **advanced degrees**) after baccalaureate degrees. Master's, doctorate, and **professional degrees** (such as a law, dentistry, veterinary medicine, or medicine) are different types of graduate degrees. Students working on advanced degrees are **graduate students** or **grad students**.

A university is a group of undergraduate colleges. Universities also **confer** (award) advanced degrees (beyond bachelor's degrees). For example, Iowa State University in Ames, Iowa, has seven undergraduate colleges and a graduate college. Universities offer a wide variety of courses and programs of study. Universities may award many or only a few types of graduate degrees. A few schools that *could* call themselves universities choose to call themselves colleges. Dartmouth College and the College of William and Mary are two examples. (I warned you the definitions were blurry!)

Doctoral universities award **doctoral degrees** (sometimes called **doctorates**). The most common doctoral degree is the **PhD**, doctor of philosophy. This puzzled me. I couldn't imagine all my professors had studied philosophy. Of course, they hadn't! In the language of universities, the term "philosophy" doesn't refer only to the field of philosophy. It refers to the word's original meaning, "love of wisdom." You can earn a PhD, doctor of philosophy, without taking a single philosophy course.

The **Carnegie Classification System** is a framework that describes the many types of US schools, in part by the amount of research conducted. **Tier I universities** have very high research activity levels. **Tier II universities** have high levels. **Tier III schools** conduct less research.

States usually own the **public colleges and universities** in the state. Elected or appointed public officials oversee the schools. Public schools get money from their state. Therefore, public schools pay attention to the wishes of the governor, legislators, and citizens of the state. Sometimes people call public schools simply **publics**. At public colleges and universities, **residents** (those who live in the state) pay lower prices than **non-residents** (people who live outside the state) pay. A few cities own public colleges. City residents may pay lower prices at these schools.

Private (independent) schools are independently owned. Sometimes people call private schools **privates**. In-state residents and out-of-state residents pay the same prices at most private schools. Occasionally private schools offer lower prices to local residents.

Some universities include both private colleges *and* public colleges. For example, at Cornell University in Ithaca, New York, the state supports three colleges (Human Ecology, Agriculture and Life Sciences, and Veterinary Medicine). Other colleges, like the College of Engineering, are private.

A **non-profit** school isn't in business to make money. Most colleges and universities are non-profit (or **not-for-profit**) organizations. If a non-profit organization takes in more money (**revenue**) than it spends (**expenses**), it must use the extra money to work toward its goals. **For-profit** organizations are in business to make money. They distribute profits to their owners. Some colleges and universities are for-profit organizations.

Colleges and universities differ in how **selective** (choosy) they are in admitting students. **Selectivity** describes the percentage of applicants a school admits. Highly-selective schools admit very few people who apply. Some schools use the term **entrance difficulty** instead of selectivity.

Transfer means to move from one college to another. Many students transfer from community colleges to four-year schools. Most students transfer after earning associate degrees. However, some students transfer to a four-year school before earning an associate degree. If they don't finish a bachelor's degree, students sometimes **reverse transfer** from a four-year to a two-year school. They can then earn an associate degree from the community college.

Career schools (technical schools, trade schools, proprietary schools, or **vocational schools)** train students to perform a particular job such as bookkeeper, medical assistant, paralegal, or computer support specialist. The programs often take one year or less to complete. Credits seldom transfer to colleges or universities. Some for-profit schools enroll many students, encourage them to get student loans, and then don't provide good job training or job placement. So, be cautious. The US Federal Trade Commission and Department of Education both recommend researching these schools carefully before attending. You can learn more by searching "vocational schools" at consumer.ftc.gov.

Some college classes are **online. Virtual learning, distance learning,** and **distributed learning** are other names for online learning. Classes that meet in person are **face-to-face** or **on-ground** classes. Nearly all colleges and universities have some online classes. Many offer full degrees online. Online learning is **synchronous** when students and instructors interact in real time. It is **asynchronous** when there isn't real-time (instantaneous) communication.

Some colleges and universities are **residential schools,** where most students live on or near campus. Others are **non-residential schools** (or **commuter schools**), where few (if any) students live on campus. Classes and other activities take place on a **campus.** Some schools have several campuses. They can be in different cities or states. Some schools even have campuses in other countries.

The **academic year** is the time when most students attend the school. In the US, it is about nine months, starting in August or September. The academic year can be different for on-campus and online classes. Most schools break up the academic year into **terms** (periods). The times between terms, when most students don't attend classes, are **breaks.** A **semester system** has two terms during the academic year. The **fall semester** might start in mid-August and continue until mid-December. The **spring semester** might start mid-January and continue through mid-May. A **trimester system** has three terms each academic year. Schools that run on semester or trimester systems have **summer sessions**. **Quarter systems** divide the academic year into four terms and count the summer as one of the terms. Some classes may not last an entire term. Some schools (for example, online schools) don't have traditional terms such as semesters or quarters.

At one time, colleges were either liberal arts *or* vocational colleges. **Liberal arts colleges** were usually small, private, residential schools. They exposed students to a broad range of classes. Students studied languages, art, philosophy, literature, politics, economics, history, and the sciences. These schools tried to develop students' general knowledge and high-level critical thinking abilities. Students generally studied at least two years before declaring a major. In contrast, **vocational colleges** focused more narrowly on career and vocational training. Students declared majors early in their college careers and focused on developing skills needed to succeed in careers. There are still liberal arts colleges and there are still vocational colleges. But today, most colleges and universities provide a mixture of liberal arts and vocational features.

You should attend a college or university accredited by an agency recognized by the US Department of Education. These agencies are private organizations that develop quality standards for higher education. Some are regional and others are national. A college periodically asks an agency to complete an **accreditation review** of a program of study. The agency then evaluates whether the program meets quality standards. Faculty and staff from other quality schools do the evaluations. If a program meets or exceeds the quality standards, it is **accredited**. The Department of Education **recognizes** (identifies and accepts) accrediting agencies. This means the department considers them reliable authorities (experts) about education and training in higher education. There is a database of accredited postsecondary institutions and programs on the department website (ope.ed.gov/accreditation). Most scholarships and other financial aid only pay for education institutions and programs included in this database. So, it's important to attend a college or university accredited by an agency recognized by the US Department of Education.

You should address most college teachers as "Professor." There are different levels of professors. However, you can address any of them as "Professor." Together, **professors** are **faculty**. At the beginning of a class, you usually get a **syllabus** (a list of books, assignments, test dates, class rules, grading policies, and due dates). It usually includes the teacher's name and contact information. If the name includes a suffix (group of letters) that indicates he or she has a doctorate (such as PhD, MD, or DVM), you may call the person "Doctor (last name)." Some college teachers don't have professor titles or hold doctoral degrees. Their titles might be instructor, lecturer, or adjunct. Teachers might tell you to address them by their first names, "Mr.," or "Ms." However, call your teachers "professor" unless you have permission to use another name. An exception to this rule is a teaching assistant. In large classes, the professor may teach once or twice a week, with another class led by a teaching assistant. **Teaching assistants** are usually graduate students working on advanced degrees. Teaching assistants are not professors or faculty. Address teaching assistants as "Ms." or "Mr. (last name)."

The head of a college is usually the **president**. If you meet the president, address him or her as "President (last name)." The person's title might also be **chancellor**. If so, call him or her "Chancellor (last name)."

One of my least favorite words in the college lingo is **matriculate**. It's been around since the 16th century, so I doubt it'll go away any time soon. It just means to enroll to earn a degree. Part Three of this book will help you determine which of the many types of schools best meets your needs. Then, in Part Four, you can decide where you want to matriculate!

CHAPTER 2 – UNDERSTAND COST AND FINANCIAL AID TERMS

A re you confused by college cost and financial aid terms? If so, you're not alone. But if you're going to get a great education at an affordable price, you have to know the language.

First, let's define the terms that describe college costs. A college charges **tuition** for instruction and basic services like libraries. Most schools set tuition one year at a time. A few schools offer flat-rate tuition. **Flat-rate tuition** guarantees that you'll pay the same tuition each year for the time normally needed to complete a degree.

Fees are charges for services that aren't part of the basic education. For example, a school might charge computer lab fees, science lab fees, student health fees, graduation fees, or job placement fees. Some fees don't apply to all students.

Room and board means housing and food. Room and board charges on student bills are for housing and food provided by the school. Some schools call this **housing and dining**. Some schools require all students to live in housing provided by the school. Others only require younger students to live on campus. Most schools have different types (and costs) of housing. Meal plans (the "board" part of "room and board") also vary in requirements, offerings, and expense.

Cost of Attendance (sometimes called the **COA**) is the estimated total cost of attending a specific school for one academic year. Costs for tuition, fees, room, board, books, supplies, and transportation are included in the cost of attendance. Dependent childcare, computer rental, study abroad fees, and loan fees are also included, if they apply. All schools provide estimates of the cost of attendance. Schools, scholarship agencies, and loan providers use this to decide the amounts of grants, scholarships, and loans.

Cost of attendance includes **direct charges** (such as tuition, fees, room, and board) that you pay to the school. It also includes **indirect costs** (books, supplies, transportation, and personal expenses) that you pay to others.

Some costs, like tuition and fees, are **fixed.** Other costs, like room, board, books, supplies, transportation, and personal expenses, are flexible. **Flexible costs** are costs that you can reduce with careful planning. Part Five of this book can help you reduce flexible costs.

Published price (sticker price) of a college or university is the price listed on the website, in pamphlets, etc. It's like the sticker price on a new car. Many people pay less after financial aid.

Net price of a college or university is the price a specific student pays to attend. It is the total annual tuition, fees, room, board, books, and other expense minus scholarships and grants provided by the federal government, the state, and the school.

Net price calculator is a feature on college websites. A net price calculator helps you estimate your net price of attending that school. (Some schools call the tools other names, such as **Personal Cost Estimator** or **Financial Aid Estimator**.) You enter your personal information (family income, etc.) into the calculator. You then get an estimate of the net price to attend if you enroll next year.

Students get financial aid to help pay for college. **Financial aid** includes scholarships, grants, Work-Study job wages, and loans. A **financial aid package** (sometimes called an **award package**) is the set of scholarships, grants, tuition waivers, fee waivers, Work-Study job wages, and loans that a school offers you to attend. **Gift aid** includes tuition waivers, scholarships, and grants that you don't pay back. **Self-help aid** includes work wages (usually from Work-Study jobs) plus loans that you have to pay back. Some people call Work-Study jobs **earned aid**.

Schools may consider how much your family can afford to pay as they decide whether to **admit** you (invite you to enroll). If a school admits students without considering their ability to pay, the school has **need-blind admissions**. Schools that consider the amount families can pay have **need-sensitive** (sometimes called **need-aware**) **admissions**.

Need-based scholarships depend on your family's finances. Schools award **merit-based scholarships** to students with strong academic skills or community service accomplishments. Many scholarships consider a combination of need and merit.

Students usually apply for scholarships. If you meet the conditions, the scholarship provider considers your application along with those of other applicants. They **award** (give) the scholarship to one or a few of the top applicants. You don't have to pay **scholarships** back.

Fellowships are like scholarships. You don't have to pay them back. Most are merit-based. Most are for graduate school, but there are some undergraduate fellowships.

Students who have an exceptional skill (for example, in art, athletics, debate, music, dance, writing, leadership, or drama) may get **talent-based scholarships**.

You can sometimes earn **service scholarships** by working in a specific profession, location, or organization.

Grants are monetary (money) awards, usually based on financial need. You don't have to repay grants. Students must normally apply for grants. If you meet the conditions of the grant and there is enough money, you typically get it. Grants for college are usually less competitive than scholarships.

Pell grants, from the US government, are the most common college grants. They depend on financial need. Most colleges take part in the Pell grant program. Another grant, for students with very high need, is the **Federal Supplemental Educational Opportunity Grant (FSEOG)** grant. Fewer colleges take part in this program. Many states and individual schools offer additional grants.

When people lose their jobs, they are sometimes eligible for **displaced worker grants**. These grants (from the state or federal government) pay for training for new careers. The training may include college.

A **tuition waiver** (or **tuition discount**) is an agreement by a school to reduce tuition. Some schools **waive** (give up) all or part of the tuition charge for exceptional students. Similarly, a **fee waiver** is an agreement to reduce (or eliminate) a fee. Tuition and fee waivers are also great types of aid, since you don't have to pay them back.

Full ride, free ride, and **full scholarship** are informal terms that describe a scholarship, waiver, and grant package that pays all of a student's college expenses. The student doesn't need to work during college, borrow money, or pay anything back. Very few students get full rides.

Student loans are funds from a government agency, lending organization (such as a bank or credit union), or school. You must pay loans back, plus interest. **Interest** is the cost of borrowing money. Student loans based on financial need sometimes charge lower interest. Subsidize means to give money to help pay for something. In this case, the government or school provides money so students can borrow at lower interest rates. Loans not based on need are generally not subsidized. Lenders therefore charge higher interest on unsubsidized loans.

Forgivable loans are debts that can be cancelled (**forgiven**). Sometimes states experience a shortage of workers in a specific field (teaching or nursing, for example). They offer forgivable loans to people who agree to work a minimum number of years in that state. Some federal programs and employers forgive student loans, too.

Jobs in a financial aid package are usually **Work-Study** jobs. The federal government contributes money for Work-Study jobs. Some states do, too. Your Work-Study award depends on your financial need, when you apply, and the money available at the school. The award is the maximum you can earn in a Work-Study job during the school year.

An **assistantship** is a paid job. **Research assistants** do research with professors. **Teaching assistants** assist professors with classes. There are many assistantships for graduate students, but fewer for undergraduates. Most go to outstanding third- and fourth-year students. Work-Study programs pay for some assistantships.

FAFSA stands for the **Free Application for Federal Student Aid**. If you want federal (and most other) need-based aid, you must complete a FAFSA for each year you attend college. It gathers information needed to decide how much need-based aid you'd get for one year of college. Most students complete it online at fafsa.ed.gov. Students can get an idea of the amount of federal aid they can get by using the **FAFSA4caster** tool on the website.

Expected Family Contribution (EFC) is a measure of your family's financial strength. Schools use the EFC to decide if you're eligible for federal student aid and how much other need-based aid you'll get. The EFC depends on family and financial information you supply on the FAFSA. This includes your family income, benefits your family receives (such as unemployment or Social Security), and **net assets** (what you own minus what you owe). The formula considers family size and the number of members who will be college students during the year. Financial need is the term used by the federal government and schools that use the FAFSA for their own (sometimes called **institutional**) grants and loans. **Financial need** is the difference between the total cost of attending the school and your expected family contribution.

Institutionally-determined need is the total price of attending a school minus what the school's financial aid administrators think you and your family can afford to pay. Colleges have different ways of evaluating need and awarding non-federal aid. Many schools use more information and calculate your expected family contribution differently than the federal government. Many schools use the **CSS/Financial Aid PROFILE** to collect information. Complete the PROFILE online at collegeboard.org.

Unmet need is the cost of attending a school minus the school-determined expected family contribution minus the financial aid offered by the school (scholarships, grants, loans, and Work-Study earnings).

If you encounter a financial aid term that you don't understand and it is not covered here, check the glossary of Edvisors.com.

So, now we have the basic terms defined. Let's start thinking about how you can get the best college education possible at an affordable price.

Chapter 3 – Start Planning – Now

How much have you planned for college? If you're reading this book, you must want to go. But you'll waste time and money if you don't think seriously, early and often about college and careers.

Learn About Careers

Spend time learning about careers *before* you start looking at colleges. That way, you'll be able to identify college majors and schools that'll prepare you well for your career.

Surprisingly, many people select college majors that don't match their interests, skills, and values. A recent report from ACT showed that only about 1/3 of high school graduates chose college majors that were good fits with their interests!

If you make a poor choice of college major, you'll waste time and money. If you decide to change your major part way through school, you'll probably have to take more courses. You might even need to transfer to a different school. Choose a major that reflects your interests, skills, and values. You'll be more likely to stay in that major and complete your degree on time.

So, how do you select a college major? If you're lucky, your high school has a good career-planning program. If you aren't involved in a career-planning program, see your school counselor. Adults can find help at one-stop career centers, workforce development centers, or student advising centers at community colleges.

There are some great tools to help you figure out which careers match your interests, skills, and values. Start by taking an interest and values inventory. An **inventory** is a questionnaire. You'll answer a series of questions. One question might ask, "Is it important to have evenings free?" Another might ask, "Do you prefer to work alone?" There are no *right* answers to these questions. Just answer the questions honestly. Your results will show careers that match your interests and values.

You should also take skill **assessments** (tests). You may already take these in school. In skill assessments, there *are* right and wrong answers. Your results show what you already know and what you're ready to learn next. These tests can help you decide which classes to take. Your skills also suggest careers in which you might do well.

Your school, one-stop career center, or workforce development center may sponsor workshops about different occupations. They may also help you arrange to **shadow** (follow and observe) someone to see what they do in their job. Some schools have internship opportunities. In an **internship,** you work part time (sometimes without pay) for a few weeks or months to learn about a job or multiple jobs.

Most career planning programs have online tools to help you learn about careers. They typically include video clips showing people doing their jobs. They include interviews in which people talk about their typical workdays. You can also find out how much jobs pay and the need for various jobs. And you'll learn about the education needed to get the jobs. Some programs even have information about jobs in your state or city.

If you can't find a counselor or career center to help with career exploration, ask your local librarian for help. Some libraries have special areas set up for college and career planning.

TRY ONLINE CAREER PLANNING TOOLS

You can use many online tools at a library or on your own. These include:

- Mynextmove.org
- Bls.gov/k12
- Careeronestop.org
- Showmethefuture.org
- Bigfuture.org
- Becomeopedia.com
- Knowhow2go.acenet.edu
- ACTprofile.org

For example, on the ACT Profile site you can take quizzes about your interests, abilities, and values. Based on your answers, you'll get personalized results. You can explore your results using interactive career and college major maps.

As you explore careers, make a list of the clusters that match your interests and skills. **Career clusters** (sometimes called **career areas** or **career paths**) are groups of careers that are similar but have different training requirements, responsibilities, and benefits.

A healthcare career cluster might include:

- Certified nursing assistant (CNA)
- Dental hygienist
- Registered nurse (RN)
- Medical doctor (MD)
- Oral surgeon

These careers are all in healthcare. But some require less than a year of training, while others require eight – or more. Day-to-day tasks, schedules, and salaries are very different.

Once you know the careers that interest you, you can start working on a plan. Think about where you are now, where you want to go, and how you're going to get there. Interest and skill assessments, plus school and work experiences, provide a sense of where you are now. Your career exploration will help you identify the career you want. Then you can start figuring out the education you'll need – and how you'll get it.

LEARN ABOUT COLLEGE

It's important for people to think about college while they're young. They need to see themselves as college students. I lived near a college when I was a child. My parents and grandparents didn't have four-year degrees. But I always knew I'd go to college. I thought about *where* I would go. But I never wondered *if* I would. Maybe you can visit a college on a school trip, with a friend, or with a parent. If so, explore the campus. Think about what college will be like for you.

There are many **pre-college programs** for middle school and high school students. Many are three- to four-week summer programs. Some are daytime programs where you go home at night. Others let you live in a college dormitory. Many have scholarships for low-income students. Check college websites to see if there are programs near your home. Your school counselor may know about programs, too.

There may also be year-round programs, such as:

- TRIO
- Upward Bound
- GearUp
- College Possible
- College Spring
- College for Every Student
- College Track
- OneGoal
- Strive for College
- The Posse Foundation
- Project Ready

Many colleges, churches, and community centers have programs for students who live nearby. These programs provide homework help, computer access, and a quiet place to study. They set up discussions with college students and visits to college campuses. If you can join a program, do it! You'll make friends who share and support your college dreams. Look for posters on bulletin boards. Talk with your counselor, teachers, and the librarian at your local library to learn what's available. If you haven't heard about any programs in your area, check the National College Access Directory (at collegeaccess.org).

If you're an excellent student in sixth or seventh grade and come from a low-income family, apply for the Jack Kent Cooke Foundation's Young Scholars Program. Students apply in 7th grade, enter the program in 8th grade, and continue through high school. This program provides some of the best college preparation and scholarships in the country. Learn more at jkcf.org.

Most schools have college planning nights for students and their parents. Sign up and go to these. Your school may even have college planning courses.

Visit with college representatives when they visit your school. Attend college fairs near your home. The website for the National Association of College Admissions Counselors (NACAC), nacacnet.org, has a section for students and parents. It includes a calendar of college fairs around the country. Your counselor will also know about nearby college fairs.

You can also learn more about college on ACT and College Board websites, actstudent.org and youcango.collegeboard.org. EdX offers The Road to Selective College Admissions online – free. It's for students in 10th and 11th grade to help with the college application process. Sign up at EdX.org.

Another good online resource is Grad Nations' online Dollars for College Toolkit (gradnation.org/learn/dollars-college-toolkit). The site is set up to help students and families understand resources that can make higher education affordable. You can download information in both English and Spanish.

If you're Hispanic, get a copy of *¡Gradúate! A Financial Aid Guide to Success* from the US Department of Education website (ed.gov). You can download free copies in English and Spanish. This brochure has tips on choosing a college. It can also help you prepare college applications.

INFORMATION FOR UNDOCUMENTED STUDENTS

¡Gradúate! A Financial Aid Guide to Success includes information for undocumented students (those who were born outside the US and are not US citizens or legal residents). The National Association of College Admissions Counselors (NACAC) website, nacacnet.org, also has financial aid information for undocumented students. These sites include information in both English and Spanish.

Other sites that provide information for undocumented students include:

- Immigrationequality.org
- National Immigration Law Center (nilc.org)
- Mexican American Legal Defense and Education Fund (maldef.org)
- Bigfuture.collegeboard.org

Your school counselor may know of other resources from your school district or state.

SUMMARY

Start learning about college and careers in middle school or sooner. Take advantage of free college career planning programs at your school, in your community, and online.

Chapter 4 – Save – as Early and as Much as You Can

Few students, other than exceptional scholars or athletes, get full rides to college. Most students and families pay for college themselves. They pay with a combination of past income (savings), current income, and future income (through loans). You can try to figure out exactly how much to save, but it's almost impossible to develop an accurate estimate. There are just too many variables. The best advice for most students and families is to start saving as early and as much as you possibly can.

Many parents struggle with saving for retirement *and* college. If your parents can't afford to save for both they should focus on retirement. Many employers match some (or all) of retirement saving contributions. So, if your parents don't contribute, they lose employer matches. They're passing up free money! Also, your parents' tax-preferred retirement savings (401Ks, 403Bs, 457s, and IRAs) don't affect most financial aid. Plus, you can borrow money for college, if needed. And you can often borrow at lower, federally-subsidized interest rates. In contrast, lenders won't loan your parents money for retirement.

How Savings Plans Work

Many people put money into a savings account or Certificate of Deposit (CD) at a bank or credit union. Or they put money in a stock or bond fund. When you do this, you're loaning your money to organizations, hoping you'll get more back than you put in. With a savings account, you get a set amount of money back. You get the original amount you deposited (called the **principal**) and an added percentage (called **interest**). For example, if you put $100 into an account that pays 2 percent interest per year and leave the money there, you'll have $102 in the account after a year. The next year the full $102 will earn interest, so you'll have $104.04 after two years. This is **compounding**.

A Certificate of Deposit (CD) works like a savings account, except you agree to keep the money in the account for a set time. If you have to take the money out early, you don't earn any interest.

In general, the longer before you start college, the more you can put into investments like stock funds. These have historically paid higher rates of return than savings accounts or CDs with guaranteed rates of return. The **rate of return** compares the amount you get back with the amount you originally put in. However, stocks and stock funds don't have guaranteed rates of return. The rate of return depends on what investors think about companies in the fund, the economy, and dividends. **Dividends** are money paid by a company to stockholders. The value of stocks can go up or down because of things you can't control. Therefore, they're riskier than savings accounts. If you're just a couple years away from college, you'll probably want to put money into investments that pay a guaranteed rate of return.

WILL SAVINGS HURT CHANCES FOR FINANCIAL AID?

You may ask, "Won't savings hurt my chances for need-based financial aid?" The answer is, "Yes, but not a lot." Under the federal financial aid formula, current income counts more than savings. Federal financial aid assumes higher-income families will use income to pay part of their children's college expenses. But the government doesn't expect families to use as much of their savings (or *any* of their retirement savings).

The financial aid formula assumes student savings are there to help pay for college. So, college savings in a parent's name will have less negative impact on need-based financial aid. When you use a financial aid need estimator, such as the

FAFSA4caster, try some different assumptions. See the impact of different types of savings on your Estimated Family Contribution.

TAX BREAK TERMS

Let's start by defining key tax terms. An **incentive** is something that motivates you to do something else. The government encourages people to do things by giving them tax breaks. There are two groups of tax incentives for higher education. The first group encourages people to *save* for college. The second group encourages people to *go* to college. This chapter covers incentives to save. Chapter 38 covers incentives to go to college.

A **tax credit** reduces the income tax you pay. A **deduction** reduces the amount of income taxed. So, a tax credit is worth more than a deduction of the same amount. Let's look at an example. Let's say your family has $50,000 annual income, is in a 15 percent tax bracket, and would normally pay $7500 in taxes. If you were eligible for a $2500 tax credit, you'd only pay $5000 in taxes. If it were a $2500 deduction, you'd pay 15 percent of $47,500, or $7125, in taxes.

TAX-FAVORED EDUCATION SAVINGS ACCOUNTS

You may want to consider an **Education Savings Account** (sometimes called an **ESA, Coverdell ESA, or Education IRA**). These plans shelter savings from income taxes. **Shelter** means you can legally avoid paying some taxes. Any taxpayer (within income limits) can put up to $2000 each year into an ESA for someone under eighteen. The **beneficiary** is the student whose college expenses will be paid by the ESA. Parents, grandparents, or teenagers with income can put money into an ESA. The total amount contributed per beneficiary can't be over $2000 each year.

ESAs have different investment options. Some savings plans adjust the mix of investments based on the time until you start college. Deposits grow tax free until you take them out for college. As long you use the money for college, you don't owe taxes when you take it out. If you decide not to go to college, you can move the savings into an ESA for another family member.

TAX-FAVORED QUALIFIED TUITION (529) PLANS

You should also consider a **Qualified Tuition Program**, often called **529 college savings accounts** because Section 529 of the tax code describes the plans. A 529 plan gives families (at any income level) a federal tax-free way to save for college. Parents, grandparents, and other relatives (or a teen with income) can fund a 529. The beneficiary must be a US citizen (or a resident alien) and must have a social security number or federal tax identification number.

There are two types of 529 plans: college savings plans and prepaid tuition plans. College savings plans let you use savings for expenses at any college. Prepaid tuition plans let you lock in future tuition at a college (or group of colleges) at preset prices. Nearly every state has a college savings plan or prepaid tuition plan. Some states offer both.

State prepaid tuition plans usually limit choices to in-state public colleges and universities. If you decide to go out of state, you don't get the full amount that you'd get if you went in state. A group of private colleges also offers a prepaid tuition plan that applies at about 270 schools. To learn more about this plan, visit privatecollege529.com.

You don't have to be a state resident to invest in its 529 plan. So, you may want to check out several plans. Plan fees and investment choices vary. However, tax benefits are usually less if you live outside the state. To get state income tax benefits, you must usually set up the 529 in that state. More than half of the states allow state income tax deductions when you contribute to 529 accounts. A few states provide tax credits for contributions. Some states also have grant and scholarship programs (limited to residents) tied to their 529 plans. The College Savings Plans Network website (collegesavings.org) provides a free guide to 529 plans and links to state 529 websites. Another source of information about plans is the Saving for College website (savingforcollege.com).

If you set up a 529, you need to consider whether the account is in your name or a parent's (or other person's) name. You'll also want to consider the effect on need-based financial aid when you take money out. The rules are complex, so read the fine print and consult with an investment or tax advisor, if needed. Also, you may lose benefits if you change 529 plans or move to a different state. Also, pay attention to 529 **commissions** (sales fees) and management fees. You can avoid paying commissions by buying directly from a fund rather than through a **broker** (sales agent).

US SAVINGS BONDS

Some people save for college using **US Savings Bonds** from the federal government. Your parents may not have to pay taxes on interest if they buy Series EE (issued 1990 or later) or Series I Savings bonds in their name(s). To get this break, they must cash the bonds to pay college expenses. To learn more about buying US savings bonds for education, check the website (treasurydirect.gov/indiv/planning/plan_education.htm).

AFFINITY AND LOYALTY PROGRAMS

Affinity or **loyalty programs** can help you save for college. One of the most popular is UPromise. You get money back when you buy through the UPromise online portal or with credit cards linked to your account. You earn on grocery, appliance, clothing, travel, restaurant, and other purchases. You can also invite relatives to join and deposit awards into your account. Your cash rewards can go into a savings account or a 529 plan. You have to spend money to earn money with these programs. However, if you're going to be buying anyway, you can save for college.

SUMMARY

Save as much as you can, as early as you can. Get the facts about different savings plans, and decide what's right for you. Remember, as hard as it is to save money for college, it'll be even harder to pay back loans. With a loan, you have to pay back the principal plus interest. And when you're done with college, there will be many things you want, or need, to buy. Every dollar you save for college is a dollar you won't have to borrow!

CHAPTER 5 – BE PREPARED

Will you be ready for college? Are you taking the right classes? Do you have top-notch reading and study skills?

Most young people say they want to get a degree from a four-year college. But according to ACT, only about one in three students graduate from high school with the skills they need to succeed in college.

Many students take the easiest route in high school. Sometimes they think high school graduation requirements are the same as college admission requirements. (They're not.) Or they may think it's better to take easy courses and get A's than to take honors classes and get B's. (It's not.) Or they may think high school grades don't matter. (They do!)

Take the most challenging courses at your high school for which you're prepared. Take at least a **core curriculum:**

- Four or more years of English (such as grammar, composition, and literature)

- Three to four years of social sciences (such as history, economics, geography, civics, and psychology)

- Three or more years of lab sciences (such as biology, chemistry, and physics)

- Three or more years of mathematics (such as Algebra I, Algebra II, geometry, and pre-calculus; not general math, business math, or consumer math classes)

Some colleges also require a semester of computer science and two to four years of foreign language (usually the same language). If you take these classes, you'll be better prepared for college and more likely to get financial aid. Some grants are *only* available to students who complete these classes.

TAKE CHALLENGING HIGH SCHOOL CLASSES

Your school may offer Advanced Placement, International Baccalaureate, Advanced International Certificate of Education, Project Lead the Way, or honors classes. Your counselor can tell you about courses at your school.

These are challenging, like college classes. Sometimes they use the same textbooks. These classes will help you learn to study, pay attention, and meet deadlines. They may even prepare you to take tests that, if you do well on them, can earn college credit. (See Chapter 8 for more information.) Also, if you do well in an advanced class, you may earn a higher weighted GPA.

The most widely available classes are **Advanced Placement** or **AP** classes. The College Board designs and oversees these courses. There are courses in more than thirty subjects. They are similar to first- and second-year college classes. To learn more about AP, visit apstudent.collegeboard.org.

The **International Baccalaureate Diploma Program (IB)** was developed for students who move from one country to another, but it is now used more broadly. It's a challenging program for the last two years of high school. It stresses critical thinking and international perspectives. About 800 schools across the US offer the program. To learn more, visit ibo.org.

The **Advanced International Certificate of Education** (AICE) is similar to IB. It is most common in Florida. Cambridge International Examinations manages the program, so some people call it called **Cambridge Academy**. Students who take qualifying classes, get good grades, and pass exams earn a Cambridge AICE Diploma. To learn more, visit cie.org.uk.

If your school offers **Project Lead the Way** (PLTW), look into it. It offers strong **STEM** (science, technology, engineering, and math) classes and projects. Rural and urban schools in every state offer PLTW. PLTW has project- and problem-based learning that let students develop solutions to real-world problems. Students tell me it's exciting, challenging, and fun! To learn more, visit pltw.org.

You may also want to dual enroll in classes that earn high school *and* college credit. Read the next chapter to learn more.

Most college admissions officers look for students who've taken challenging courses, even if their grades are a little lower than those who took easier classes. You're also more likely to get scholarships and grants if you've taken tough classes. And people who take the toughest high school classes are more likely to stay in college and graduate, according to Cliff Adelman, a US education expert. So, take the most demanding courses your school offers.

GET YOUR TEACHERS AND COUNSELOR ON YOUR TEAM

Make sure your parents, counselor, and teachers know you plan to go to college. Even if your family has a hard time paying rent, don't let anyone think you aren't "college material." When teachers think students don't want to (or can't) go to college, they treat them differently. For example, ACT research shows that high school teachers are more likely to teach high-level reading skills to college-bound students than they are to teach them to students who they think aren't going to college. So, tell your teachers that you're going to college!

Sports psychologists teach athletes to imagine perfect dives, perfect field goals, or perfect passes. Do the same. Picture yourself as a successful college student. Then ask your parents, teachers, and counselor to help you turn that image into a reality.

Look for the teachers who challenge students, rather than the easy ones. Push yourself to do your best. If you don't understand something, ask questions. If your school or library has a homework help line, use it. Work hard in high school. In the end, you'll be glad you did.

AVOID REMEDIAL CLASSES, IF POSSIBLE

You want to enter college ready to take credit-bearing classes. **Credit-bearing classes** are college-level classes that count toward your degree. Many colleges won't accept you if you're aren't ready for credit-bearing classes. Other colleges may accept you, but they'll make you take **remedial** (sometimes called **developmental, basic skills**, or **pre-college classes**) before you can start taking credit-bearing classes.

More than half of college students take remedial coursework. It's wonderful that remedial classes are available for people who need them. However, who wants to pay college tuition to learn what you could have learned in high school? In addition, if you need remedial classes, some schools might admit you, but will not consider you for most financial aid. Many grants and scholarships will *only* cover classes that count toward a degree. And you don't want to use up your savings on classes that don't count toward graduation, either. So, try to avoid remedial classes.

TAKE A REFRESHER COURSE

You may be a nontraditional college student, an adult 25 or older who is starting or resuming college. Older students have some extra things to consider, as they get ready for college. For example, what if you already graduated high school and you didn't take a core curriculum? If you're in that situation, check to see what high school classes the colleges you're considering require. If you're just one or two courses short, you may be able to get the requirement waived. Call the admissions office to find out. If they won't waive the requirement, you may need to start at a community college. Baccalaureate colleges often don't require the same high school classes for transfer students that they require for freshmen. Transfer decisions often depend on the college courses you've taken and the grades you earned.

You may need remedial classes to provide a solid foundation for credit-bearing college courses. However, if you took the class earlier, perhaps you can remember it if you take a refresher class. Refresher courses are available at community colleges, over the Internet, and through your local library. Khanacademy.org and hippocampus.org offer free videos about specific topics in math, science, English, and other subjects. These are good refreshers for anyone.

If you think you need a refresher course, try to take it *before* you take college entrance and placement tests. That way you may avoid remedial classes. The ACT, SAT, ACT Compass, ACCUPLACER, and ALEKS are some of the tests used to place students in classes. If you can take a refresher class and remember the skills, you may do better on these placement tests and can possibly start in a credit-bearing class.

SHARPEN YOUR READING SKILLS

If your reading skills aren't top notch, do something about it – now. College can be difficult and frustrating if you have low reading skills. Poor and slow readers find they can't keep up with the reading pace of college. If you're having trouble reading this book (written at eighth grade reading levels), try to improve your skills before you start college. Ask your guidance counselor or favorite teacher if there are resources at your school to help improve reading. Most schools have reading specialists or volunteer reading tutors.

IF YOU HAVE A LEARNING DISABILITY, FIND SUPPORT

If you have a learning disability, make sure you get the right support in high school, to help you be ready for college. The National Center for Learning Disabilities can help you find the right resources. Their website provides detailed information about how to get an **Individualized Education Program (IEP)**. An IEP helps your school develop accommodations for your learning disability. It also helps you, your teachers, parents, and other people work together to help you be ready for college. Visit ncld.org to learn about these resources.

If you have a diagnosed learning disability, you'll also want to apply for any accommodations you need for college admissions and placement tests, such as the ACT and SAT. You will probably be able to get similar accommodations to those you have in high school testing situations. Allow extra time beyond what is normally required to register for these tests. You'll need to supply detailed information about your diagnosis and the testing accommodations made by your high school. You can learn more about the application process at the ACT and SAT websites, actstudent.org and collegeboard.org. Search "testing accommodations."

When you're ready to look at colleges, look for those that offer strong support. Almost all colleges and universities provide some services and accommodations. Schools must do this to comply with the Americans with Disabilities Act (ADA). But some schools offer much more support than others do. To learn about schools that offer exceptional services, get a copy of Peterson's *Colleges with Programs for Students with Learning Disabilities or Attention Deficit Disorders*. Another good book is the Princeton Review's *K and W Guide to Colleges for Students with Learning Differences*. Your guidance counselor may have copies, or your local librarian may be able to order them through interlibrary loan.

SUMMARY

Take the toughest classes possible as you prepare for college, and study hard. If you've been out of school for several years or you've forgotten some information, take a refresher course online or at a local community college before taking college placement tests. Hopefully, you can take credit-bearing classes right away in college and be on your way to earning your   degree.

CHAPTER 6 – DUAL ENROLL IN HIGH SCHOOL AND COLLEGE

Did you know you could earn college credits while in high school? Students do this through **dual enrollment, joint enrollment, concurrent enrollment, early college**, and **middle college** programs. High school juniors and seniors (and even younger students) can take part. Courses earn both college and high school credit. College-level courses, from English and foreign languages to mathematics, computer science, and social sciences, are available for dual enrollment credit.

If you live in a city, you might enroll in a middle college (on a college campus) or an early college high school. There are about 250 public early college high schools in the US. There are early college programs in about half the states, and new programs are starting every year. Some of these programs are only open to low-income, first-generation, or minority students. (You're a **first-generation student** if your parents never went to college or went, but didn't finish.) Some programs target **first-in-the-family students**. These students don't have parents, brothers, or sisters who've gone to college.

Middle college and early college high schools usually have small classes, great teachers, and extra tutoring available. Many operate year-round to provide extra learning opportunities. They have good records of getting students prepared to enroll in, and graduate from, college. You get up to two years of college credit – free. Plus, counselors can help you find scholarships that pay all or part of your remaining college. If you qualify for a middle college or an early college high school, go for it! To learn more about early college programs and find one in your area, visit earlycolleges.org.

Other dual enrollment programs are at regular high schools or nearby college campuses. Some dual-enrollment programs are year-round, so you can take classes in summer, too. College faculty teach (or supervise) these classes. Some classes are online (especially in rural areas). Community colleges or state universities offer most programs. So, tuition prices are reasonable. In fact, your local school district or state may pay your entire tuition. Students usually have to pay for books and lab fees. And your family usually has to arrange and pay for transportation. But some programs give free or low-cost bus or subway passes to students, and carpooling is common.

Some dual enrollment programs are **career academies** organized around career clusters. Common career clusters are health sciences, advanced manufacturing, construction technology, and computer technologies. A program might offer high school classes (math, English, science, etc.), but the problems and assignments focus on careers. Many students find these classes more interesting than traditional classes. For example, construction technology students get excited about geometry, algebra, and physics when they use them to design a house. These types of academies also include experiential learning. Rather than talk about building a house, you might get to build one!

School districts vary in how much they promote dual enrollment. Sometimes the college and high school work like one school. But in other places, you might have to dig for information. Start at the admissions office of your local community college. High school guidance counselors may also provide good information. However, sometimes high school staff members don't help much. Dual enrollment programs often mean extra work and less money for high schools. So, some high school administrators aren't thrilled with the programs, and they're not eager to have their students involved.

Once you get information about dual enrollment programs in your area, you must meet entrance requirements and deadlines. You usually need good scores on a standardized test. They also require a strong grade point average (GPA) and recommendations from teachers. You must also have your parent's permission.

A word of caution: *before* you sign up for dual enrollment, find out if dual enrollment courses earn credit at the colleges you're considering. Most community colleges and in-state public universities will accept dual enrollment credits. However, schools may limit the number of transfer credits. Some will apply the credits only as elective courses. Other schools may not transfer *any* dual credits. Credits are more likely to transfer if college faculty members teach the classes.

Sometimes students must choose between Advanced Placement (AP) and dual enrollment classes. Many high schools let students take both types of classes. But others make students choose one route or the other. It's a tough choice, since both can be good options. Think about where you'll learn the most. Find out which classes are likely to earn college credit at the colleges where you're applying. And remember, just because you complete an Advanced Placement class *doesn't* mean you'll get college credit for it. You still have to take and do well on difficult end-of-course exams. And each college makes its own decisions about awarding college credit for high scores on these exams. (Read Chapter 8 to learn more.)

I met a young man who developed an excellent strategy for the AP versus dual enrollment issue. He was interested in becoming a medical doctor. His high school allowed students to take both types of classes. So, he took a variety of dual enrollment classes with healthcare emphasis. But he also took AP biology, AP chemistry, and AP Spanish. He was able to get hands-on medical experience in his dual enrollment classes, plus about thirty dual enrollment college credits. He knew that the dual enrollment credits would transfer to three of his top choice colleges. At the same time, he got a very solid understanding of biology, chemistry, and Spanish in his AP classes. If he did well on the AP exams, most of his college choices would award credit. However, even if he didn't score high enough on the exams, he knew he'd have a good understanding of these important subjects and be well prepared for college classes.

Summary

If you can enroll in a free or low-cost dual credit program, it's usually a good idea. It's a great way to save up to two years of college expenses. If you must choose between dual enrollment and Advanced Placement classes, think about where you'll learn the most. Find out which classes are likely to earn credit at the colleges you're considering.

CHAPTER 7 – MAKE THE MOST OF ENTRANCE EXAMS

Are you going to take the ACT, the SAT, or both? Almost all four-year colleges require results from a standardized admissions test such as the ACT or SAT. So, you'll probably want to take one, or both, of these exams.

Many people are afraid of college entrance exams. You shouldn't be. Almost nobody *likes* to take tests. Most people don't look forward to going to the doctor, either. However, we know it's important to go and get a regular checkup. A doctor checks your pulse, blood pressure, weight, etc. to assess your health status. The ACT and SAT check the status of your academic skills. With your test results, the ACT and SAT websites can help you find college majors and schools that fit your needs. And your test results help a college place you in appropriate first-year college classes.

TAKE ACT ASPIRE OR THE PSAT

Most high school students take the ACT or SAT during their junior year. But ACT and SAT also have tests for younger students. ACT calls their test ACT Aspire. SAT calls their test PSAT. These tests may be free at your school.

The results of ACT Aspire for 8th grade and early high school give you an idea of your strengths and areas you need to work on, to be ready for college. ACT Aspire results can help you explore college majors with online resources.

You may have to pay to take the PSAT. You sometimes take it on a Saturday. You may also need to go to a different school to take it. If you're a high school sophomore or junior, talk to your guidance counselor about it. Your counselor can help you sign up. Your counselor may even get you a fee waiver, to take the test for less (or even free). PSAT results help you plan for college using a special website.

TAKE THE ACT OR SAT

During your junior year, take the ACT, the SAT, or both. Most students register in the winter to take one or both tests the following spring. Some schools have all students take the ACT or SAT on a school day during junior year. Many students take the tests again senior year. Register online, ahead of the deadline. Most colleges will use either the ACT or SAT for admissions and course placement. But the tests are different. You may do better on one than the other. If you take classes between tests, you may also score a little higher the second time.

Colleges, universities, and scholarship agencies use ACT and SAT results to help identify students who are good matches to their programs. You decide if you want to receive information from colleges and scholarship organizations. Read the ACT and SAT privacy policies to learn more.

Most test questions are multiple-choice. Some schools also require an essay-style writing test. ACT's writing test is optional (at extra cost). The SAT currently includes a writing test. The SAT writing test will also be optional, starting in 2016. If you don't take a writing test, you'll save about $15.00. But, if you need a writing test for any college, sign up for it. You can't go back later and *just* take a writing test. So, figure out what you need, and sign up for the right test.

Some four-year schools also require SAT II Subject Tests. Since the ACT includes a science section (and the SAT doesn't), some schools (Duke, Tufts, Boston College, and others) don't require SAT II scores if you take the ACT. So, check out what schools require, and just take the tests you need. If the ACT satisfies all your test needs, don't waste time or money taking SAT II tests.

Students don't need the SAT or ACT for most community colleges. Students take another placement exam such as ACT Compass, ACCUPLACER, or ALEKS. You don't sign up for these like the ACT or SAT. The school usually arranges testing on campus or online. These exams help place you in the best courses for your current skill levels. Community colleges can also often use ACT or SAT results, if you already have them.

If you take the SAT and the ACT just once each, you'll spend about $100. ACT and the College Board are both non-profits that aren't out to make money off poor students. Therefore, they offer free tests to low-income eleventh and twelfth graders. The College Board waives fees for low-income students to take the SAT on two different test dates. They'll also waive fees for two SAT II exams. ACT also waives fees for two test dates. If your family qualifies for free or reduced-price school lunches, you're eligible for waivers. You may also qualify if you're in a federal, state, or local college prep program for low-income students (for example, TRIO programs). You may qualify if your family receives public assistance, or if you live in federally-subsidized public housing or a foster home. Your school counselor should have the fee waiver forms. If you're eligible, take advantage of these waivers. They can save you more than $250.

Everyone can save money on these tests. Start by registering before the regular test deadline. (Both ACT and SAT charge extra for late registrations.) Apply online, to save the cost of postage stamps. Know if colleges require writing scores and if you need SAT II subject tests. Both ACT and SAT charge extra if you change test dates or change test centers. So, register on time and stick to your test date and test center.

ACT and SAT will send free score reports to four schools (or scholarship organizations) *each* time you test. But it's *only* free if you provide the information when you register (or within a few days after Saturday SAT test dates). They charge (a lot) for additional score reports ordered later. They charge even more if you need score reports sent in a rush. So, know the schools (and scholarship organizations) where you want scores sent. Include this information when you register for the test(s).

Since ACT and SAT give you four free score reports every time you test, take advantage of them. If you plan to test more than once, send score reports to safety schools (where you're almost certain to be accepted) the first time you test. When you take later tests, send scores to more selective schools and scholarship organizations. (If you get a much higher score, you can always order an additional score report to send to safety schools. You might want to do this, for example, if the safety school might offer merit-based financial aid, based in part on high scores.)

SKIP PRICEY TEST PREP

You need to do your best on these exams. However, students waste money on expensive test prep. That same money can pay for tuition, room, and board in college. Your goal shouldn't be to "get in" to the most selective college. Your goal should be to enroll where you'll do well, and start in classes that match your skills. You want courses that will take you from your current knowledge to the next level. So, the best test prep for college exams is to study hard and do well in high school classes.

Before test day, make sure you're familiar with instructions and types of questions. Know the format of the test. Also, know the rules (like the calculator you can use, and whether the test penalizes for guessing). The bargain place to learn this is the company website. For the ACT, go to actstudent.org. For the SAT, go to collegeboard.org. You can get loads of free information on these websites. You can take free, timed practice tests and get results. The SAT even has videos from Khan Academy that show how to solve different problems. So skip the pricey test prep. Get it free!

Some high schools offer free or low-cost test prep classes. Typically, they're in the evening or after school. Counselors often organize these sessions and students pay little or nothing. Some PTAs, Boys and Girls Clubs, and other teen organizations also offer free or low-cost test prep. If your school has a college center (sometimes called a **Go Center**), look for free test prep classes.

Get ready ahead, so you aren't rushed and distracted on test day. Remember to do each of the following:

- Know how to get to the test center.
- Make sure your calculator battery is charged.
- Get a good night's sleep.
- Eat a good breakfast.
- Make sure you have your photo ID.
- Allow plenty of time to get to the test site.
- Relax and do your best.

UNDERSTAND YOUR TEST RESULTS

When you get test results, spend time understanding them. Don't just look at the numbers. The reports tell you so much more! For example, the ACT provides good information about the types of careers and college majors that match your skills and interests.

Students used to select a college without knowing their major or career plans. They spent the first couple of years exploring. They decided on a major about year three. But that model has changed. You want to get the highest quality of education, in the shortest amount of time and at the least cost. So, understand your career interests and focus on college majors *before* you select a school. Use career-planning tools like those described in Chapter 3 plus test results to identify promising career clusters. If you can focus on careers and majors before you start college, you'll save time and money.

SUMMARY

Register in the fall of junior year to take the ACT and/or the SAT in the spring. Know if colleges need a writing test. Register on time. Take advantage of test fee waivers, if you're eligible. Register to send the free score reports to schools and scholarship organizations where you plan to apply.

Use free online tools to get ready for tests. Know the question formats and rules. Complete timed practice tests and review results. Prepare for test day, and get a good night's sleep the night before.

Review test results carefully. Learn all you can about the best careers and college majors that match your skills and interests. Use results to help you find the best college and career for you.

Chapter 8 – Get Credit for What You Already Know

Do you already know things taught in college classes? Do you wish you could get college credit for what you already know? Maybe you can.

Many people earn college credit before they take a single college class. Young people usually get credit for high scores on special exams. Adults or teens who are fluent in a second language can often earn college credit through exams. Adults can get credit for experience, sometimes even without exams.

It isn't simple to get college credit for prior learning. But it can save you time – and money. If you get credit for just one course at a state university, you can save several hundred dollars. It can be worth thousands at private schools.

Start by finding and understanding policies of schools you're considering. Colleges (and individual departments or majors) have specific rules and procedures for granting credit for prior learning. Some colleges want higher exam scores than others. A university may give you credit for some majors, but not for others. Many schools award credit for electives rather than allowing credit for required courses. And almost all schools place a limit on the number of credits they'll award for prior learning.

Some colleges don't award credit at all. They place students in more advanced classes instead. Some give credit for lower level courses skipped. For example, my test scores let me skip a basic chemistry course in college. If I earned an A or B in the advanced course, I earned credit for both courses. So, I got six credits rather than three. And I saved time and money I'd have spent on the basic class.

Most colleges list credit-for-prior-learning policies on their websites. Look under "credit for prior learning," "credit by examination," "advanced standing," or "advanced placement." Some list policies under "prior-learning assessment," "credit for competencies," or "competency-based credit." Read materials carefully. Then communicate directly with the colleges and departments where you're applying. Make sure you have complete and up-to-date information.

ADVANCED PLACEMENT

For young people, Advanced Placement (AP) and the International Baccalaureate (IB) Diploma are the most common ways to earn credit for prior learning.

Advanced Placement is the most widely used program. There are courses and exams in more than thirty subjects. Some people assume that, when they take Advanced Placement classes, they automatically receive college credit. That is <u>not</u> correct. AP classes earn high school credit. To earn college credit students must take an exam at the end of class, do well on the exam, *and* attend a college that grants credit for qualifying AP scores. According to the College Board, more than 90 percent of US colleges and universities grant credit and/or higher course level placement for qualifying AP exam scores.

High schools that offer AP classes offer the tests in early May. If your school doesn't offer AP exams, you'll need to arrange (by March 1) to take the test(s) at another school. Home-schooled students can also arrange to take tests. You can find out how on the College Board website (apstudent.collegeboard.org). You can get free test prep for AP exams on this website. EdX.org also has free online, self-paced classes to help you prepare for AP exams.

AP exams aren't cheap. The full price is close to $100 per test. However, the College Board offers reduced fees for lower-income students. Plus, many school districts and states pay all or part of exam fees. Check with your guidance counselor or

AP coordinator to learn about discounts. For more about AP, visit the College Board website's AP section at apstudent.collegeboard.org.

THE INTERNATIONAL BACCALAUREATE AND AICE

Some colleges and universities offer credit to anyone who has an International Baccalaureate (IB) Diploma or Advanced International Certificate of Education (AICE) Diploma. Even more schools give credit to those with high scores on exams. For more information about the International Baccalaureate Diploma Program and links to schools that award college credit based on IB exam scores, visit ibo.org. To learn more about the AICE, visit cie.org.uk.

ASSESSMENTS OF PRIOR LEARNING AND COMPETENCY-BASED EXAMS

Prior learning assessment (PLA) programs target adult learners. Home-schooled students and students who attend schools without AP, IB, or AICE also use them. If you can show you have specific skills, knowledge, and abilities, you can earn college credit. It doesn't matter where you learned it. It can be through reading, home schooling, noncredit adult courses, travel, hobbies, on-the-job training, volunteer work, free online courses, or military service. Colleges use tests, evaluations of student portfolios, and recommendations from the American Council on Education to assess skills, knowledge, and abilities.

There are also several nationwide exams. Unlike AP or IB exams, they aren't tightly coordinated with specific high school courses. Some people call these **competency-based exams (CBE)**. Those who are fluent in a second language often earn college credit by scoring well on these exams.

Some schools base entire degrees on the student's ability to demonstrate skills and knowledge in a field. Students often start in these degree programs with credit granted for their prior learning. (Read Chapter 21 to learn more.)

More than 2900 colleges use the **College-Level Examination Program (CLEP)** from the College Board. There are more than thirty CLEP exams. Topics include business, science, math, composition, literature, history, social science, and foreign languages. Tests are similar to final exams in college courses. You can take exams year-round at test centers (at colleges and universities) throughout the country. Some exam centers only allow testing by their own students. CLEP exams cost about $80 each. Military personnel can take CLEP exams free on many bases. They pay a registration fee when they take exams at a college or university CLEP center. Some spouses and civilian employees also get free testing on military bases. For more information about CLEP exams, visit the College Board website (clep.collegeboard.org).

DSST is similar to CLEP. It provides more than thirty exams in various subjects including social science, business, math, applied technology, humanities, and physical science. About 2000 US colleges award credit for passing scores. You can take the tests at campus testing centers. Some sites only allow their own students to test. Many military bases also give these tests. You can download free information about DSST and get test preparation for some exams (for a fee) at getcollegecredit.com.

There are about 50 **UExcel Exams (Excelsior College Exams)**. They include business, education, arts, sciences, nursing, social sciences, history, and natural sciences. Excelsior College and hundreds of others award credit for passing scores. You can take them at Pearson VUE Centers and on some military bases. Military personnel can take the exams free at some test centers. Test prep materials are available (some at no charge) on the Excelsior College website, excelsior.edu.

You may also get college credit for training and exams you've already taken. The **American Council on Education (ACE) College Credit Recommendation Service (CREDIT)** evaluates and recommends college credit for courses, certifications, apprenticeships, and exams. Business, labor, government, and professional organizations provide the exams. ACE also evaluates and recommends credit for formal training provided by the military.

More than 2000 colleges and universities consider ACE CREDIT recommendations. Students who want to see if ACE has reviewed a program and recommends college credit can look at acenet.edu/NationalGuide. The website lists about 35,000 course evaluations and credit recommendations. If a course or exam you've completed is in this guide, you can pay ACE to send a transcript to your school. (A **transcript** is an official listing of courses you've taken and the grades you've earned. It also lists honors and degrees you've received.) However, just because ACE recommends credit, *doesn't* mean every college (or department) will accept the recommendations and grant credit.

The **National College Credit Recommendation Service (NCCRS)** has a similar service. More than 1500 colleges and universities will consider granting college credit based on NCCRS recommendations. Visit www.nationalccrs.org to see courses covered by this system.

Did you know there were so many ways to get credit for what you already know? Credit for prior learning has been around for decades. But it's becoming more common, and colleges are becoming more open about their policies.

Getting credit for prior learning takes effort. It's complex and sometimes frustrating. Find out the exams used by the colleges and departments you're considering *before* you spend money to take exams. Also, learn any other requirements for receiving college credit. Some schools have counseling services to help students get credit for prior learning. But these services usually aren't available until after you enroll.

Kaplan's Open College recently introduced a free online Learning Recognition Course. It is an eight-module, self-paced course. Students develop a portfolio that describes and organizes the learning they have acquired on the job, through volunteer work, travel, etc. Students also examine their future goals. At the end of this course, students have the option to submit their portfolios for evaluation. Faculty members determine whether the learning, as described and documented, is college level. There is no fee for the course, but there *is* a fee for the evaluation. You may want to consider completing this course to help guide your thinking about prior learning. Learn more at opencollege.kaplan.com. (If you enroll, expect to get phone calls and emails trying to convince you to enroll in other Kaplan classes.) I'm hopeful other colleges will develop similar online portals to help students determine the credit they can receive for prior learning.

As complicated as credit for prior learning is, think about the potential savings. If you get thirty college credits, the equivalent of about ten classes, it could save you a year in college. That can easily mean $15,000 or more in savings at an in-state school – and $50,000 or more at a private one.

SUMMARY
You can earn college credit for what you already know. Young people usually get credit for high scores on special exams. Adults get credit for experience, sometimes even without exams. It isn't simple to get college credit for prior learning. But it can save you time – and money. But remember, credit for prior learning should be only one factor in your choice of schools.

CHAPTER 9 – GET AN ACCELERATED DEGREE

If you're well prepared and disciplined, you can graduate faster. Many students graduate quickly by getting credit for prior learning, as discussed in the last chapter. But it's tough to handle on your own. It's easier to enroll in a program designed to graduate students quickly.

PROGRAMS FOR WORKING ADULTS

Students who work full time often take fewer classes at a time and therefore take longer to graduate. However, some colleges have programs that let people work full time and still earn degrees quickly. The Program for Adult College Education (PACE) at Berkeley City College in California is one of the best. PACE students take first-year classes as a **cohort** (group). Everyone takes the same set of first-year classes together. Some schools call these **locked classes**. This makes study groups and team projects easier. Classes are in the evenings. Counselors, tutors, and financial aid advisors are available on Saturdays. Saturday workshops include career exploration, scholarship opportunities, and transfer planning. During the second year, students take classes in their majors. If you work full time and want an associate degree, see if a community college near you offers this type of program.

Some baccalaureate schools also offer accelerated degrees for working adults. For example, Mount Mercy University in Cedar Rapids, Iowa, offers an accelerated program. Classes meet one night each week or on Saturday mornings for five or ten weeks. This allows students to focus on one class at a time instead of juggling several classes at once. Students in this program earn their degrees in one of twelve majors.

PROGRAMS OPEN TO RECENT HIGH SCHOOL GRADUATES

A few community colleges offer programs that allow full-time students to earn an associate degree in one year. The programs are usually limited to recent high school graduates. For example, Indiana's Ivy Tech Associate Accelerated Program (ASAP) is limited to students 21 or younger. These programs require good high school grades, attendance records, and references. Most of the programs are cohort programs, where students move through courses in a specific sequence as a group.

Some US colleges and universities have programs that let full-time students complete bachelor's degrees in just three years. These programs often let students register early and provide special advisors who keep them on track. They're best for those who are motivated and well prepared. Students must usually be sure of their major and willing to work hard. Students who have done well on Advanced Placement (AP) and International Baccalaureate (IB) exams should also consider them. For example, University of North Carolina (Greensboro) offers a UNC in Three program to undergrads with at least twelve credits from AP, IB, or other exams.

More than a dozen Ohio universities offer three-year degrees. The University of Akron, Miami University of Ohio, Ohio State University, and University of Toledo all have them. Other schools that offer three-year bachelor's degrees include:

- American University (in Washington, DC)
- Hartwick College (in upstate New York)
- Purdue University (in Indiana)
- Southern New Hampshire University
- Southern Oregon University
- Wesleyan University (in Connecticut)

Many other colleges and universities are developing accelerated bachelor's degree programs.

BACHELOR'S PLUS GRADUATE DEGREES

Some accelerated programs combine bachelor's degrees with professional degrees (such as medicine, law, pharmacy, or master of business administration). These are **dual-degree, combined-degree,** or **concurrent-degree** programs. Students usually complete most of their bachelor's degree in three years, and then start the professional degree. Students save one or more years, avoiding tuition, fees, housing, and book costs. Plus, they can start jobs earlier.

Clark University (in Worcester, Massachusetts) offers a five-year combined bachelor's/master's program. Clark's Fifth Year Free program lets high-performing, ambitious students earn master's degrees the year after they get Clark bachelor's degrees. Students just pay for room, board, and books during the fifth year. About 25 percent of Clark undergraduates take part.

Earning an undergraduate degree plus an MD degree usually takes about eight years of school. About thirty US schools offer combined undergraduate and MD degrees. These take six or seven years to complete. For example, Penn State offers a six-year Accelerated Premedical-Medical Program (BS/MD). In a seven-year program at Tulane University (in New Orleans, Louisiana), students complete undergrad and medical degrees in six years, with a year of public service between the degrees.

More than 25 law schools offer six-year accelerated programs. Most, like Creighton (in Omaha, Nebraska) are 3+3 programs, where students complete an undergraduate degree in three years and law school during the next three years. A few, including Northwestern University (in Chicago, Illinois) are 4+2 programs.

According to a 2012 *US News* survey, nearly 40 percent of bachelor's degree graduates start an advanced degree within five years. If you know you want an advanced degree, a dual-degree program may make sense. Most business and law schools prefer students work a few years after college. Many of the combined degree programs require internships, so students gain high-quality work experience before receiving their advanced degrees.

SUMMARY

An increasing number of US schools offer three-year bachelor's degrees. Some accelerated programs combine bachelor's degrees with professional degrees (such as medicine, law, pharmacy, or master of business administration). Consider an accelerated degree if you're motivated, well prepared, sure of your major, and willing to work hard.

Combined degree programs save time and money. Every college year saved is a year you won't have to pay for. And you can launch your career and earn money a year sooner.

CHAPTER 10 – START AT A COMMUNITY COLLEGE

Should you go to a community college? About half of today's college students do. It's an easy way to cut expenses. Even with recent large tuition increases, community colleges are still a bargain. According to the College Board's *2014 Trends in College Pricing*, published community college full-time tuition and fees averaged about $3350 per year for 2014-2015. Some states even offer free community college. For example, beginning in 2015, all Tennessee high school graduates can get two years of tuition-free community college. In addition, according to the American Association of Community Colleges, almost half of community college students get financial aid. Community colleges are especially affordable if you can live with a relative and avoid housing costs.

Teachers are another great part of community colleges. You'll find most teachers doing exactly what they want to do – teach. In contrast, many university professors would rather do research or work with graduate students than teach first- and second-year students. Community colleges also have smaller classes than large universities.

If you need refresher or remedial classes, community colleges have more available and at lower costs. Some community colleges also offer **co-requisite classes** rather than non-credit-bearing remedial classes. In a co-requisite system, students take a credit-bearing class plus an extra support class. For example, suppose you have low math placement scores. In a co-requisite system, you would not take a remedial math class. Instead, you'd take a credit-bearing introductory math class and a partner support section. So, you'd pay for one class, financial aid would apply, and you'd get college credit if you earned a passing grade.

WORKFORCE TRAINING PROGRAMS

Community colleges provide strong workforce training programs. These can be two-year associate degree programs, apprenticeship programs, or shorter certificate programs. They provide entry-level career training right out of high school. They can also help adults upgrade job skills or change fields. They lead to jobs like air traffic controller, electrician, or welder. You can also train to become a radiation therapist, registered nurse, or medical records technician. You can become an agribusiness specialist, advanced manufacturing technician, culinary arts specialist, or auto technician. These **middle skill** jobs pay well. According to Georgetown University's Center on Education and the Workforce, nearly 30 percent of Americans with associate degrees earn more than those with baccalaureate degrees. Training programs also target local needs, so students have good local opportunities. When you consider how much less these programs cost and how much less time they require (compared to a bachelor's degree), they're good options to consider.

However, credits earned in these programs often won't transfer or apply toward a bachelor's degree. There are some exceptions. For example, some schools offer **Applied Bachelor's** degrees. If want an Applied Bachelor's degree in construction management, you might get a two-year construction technology associate degree. You'd then transfer to a four-year school and take **upper-level** (junior and senior) courses like project management, estimating, and accounting, and then earn your Applied Bachelor's degree. However, these degrees are rare. So, if your goal is to get a bachelor's degree, make sure your community college credits will transfer to a four-year school.

FIRST TWO YEARS TOWARD A BACHELOR'S DEGREE

The second major purpose of community colleges is to provide the first two years of a bachelor's degree. Students earn an associate degree and then transfer to a baccalaureate school.

However, if it's such a smart strategy, why don't all students start at a community college? There are many reasons. Some schools aren't good at preparing and helping students transfer. According to the Community College Research Center, eight in ten students who start at a community college say they intend to earn a bachelor's degree. However, only two in ten transfer to four-year schools. And only one in ten earns a bachelor's degree within six years.

To make your transfer go smoothly, the community college needs clear agreements with the school where you'll transfer. Community colleges usually have articulation agreements with several baccalaureate schools. **Articulation agreements** spell out which credits transfer and the conditions. Sometimes the schools even have **joint applications**. You apply to both at the same time. If accepted, you know you can attend the four-year school after community college.

Some students dual-enroll and take classes at both schools. For example, a student at the University of Iowa may also be taking classes at Kirkwood Community College's nearby campus. This works well if you meet the tougher entrance requirements of the baccalaureate school. However, dual enrollment *could* keep you from getting financial aid. If you're a part-time student at two colleges, you may not be eligible for aid restricted to full-time students.

Almost all community colleges have articulation agreements with public universities in their states. About 1/4 of the states have statewide course numbering systems. So, it's easy to know what transfers. In some states all public schools have common **general education** (sometimes called **gen ed** or **core**) courses. These courses are required for most bachelor's degrees.

Most community colleges also have articulation agreements with private schools. Florida community colleges have agreements with about thirty privates, as well as eleven state universities. Drake University, a private university in Des Moines, Iowa, has articulation agreements with nine Iowa community colleges. Students can check online to see exactly which courses transfer. Drake also completes official transfer of credit evaluations for students as soon as they apply for admission. So, students know what transfers *before* they accept Drake admission offers. Community college transfer students are also eligible for generous financial aid.

Bradley University (in Peoria, Illinois) is another private school that does a great job with transfers. Bradley has Course Equivalency Guides for more than forty other schools. These help students plan transfers. And transfer students who've done well at their previous school (3.5 or higher GPA) qualify for $5000 scholarships.

Some states have scholarships for community college graduates who transfer to in-state four-year schools. There are also some great independent scholarships for community college transfer students. The Jack Kent Cooke Foundation's Undergraduate Transfer Scholarship is one. It's a need-based scholarship, which provides up to $30,000 each year. It covers expenses for the final two to three years of a bachelor's degree. Learn more at jkcf.org.

You can even get an associate degree at a community college, and then transfer to an Ivy League school. Yale, Stanford, Cornell, and Harvard all recruit exceptional community college graduates. Other highly-selective schools, such as Smith, Wellesley, Mount Holyoke, Bates, and Vassar, do, too.

Students normally identify a local community college, and then figure out the four-year schools with transfer agreements. But you can work from the other direction, too. You can decide where you want to get your bachelor's degree, and then figure out which community colleges have articulation agreements. For example, you could go to the Syracuse University website (syr.edu) and search on "community college articulation agreements." You'd find that Syracuse (in upstate New York) has transfer agreements with about 25 community colleges. A few are as far away as California!

Some community colleges have agreements that let students earn their *entire* bachelor's degree on the community college campus. Some schools call these **hybrid programs**. For example, students can earn an associate degree in engineering from Houston Community College (HCC), and then enroll at University of Texas (UT, Tyler). Students earn a UT bachelor's degree in engineering. But they can take all classes on the HCC campus in Houston.

BE SUCCESSFUL STARTING AT A COMMUNITY COLLEGE

Look for a community college that has a good record of transferring students to the school where you want to get your bachelor's degree. Talk to the transfer advisors at <u>both</u> schools. Plan your program of study carefully. For example, courses that receive transfer credit for one major may not get credit in another. A community college math course might transfer with credit to a teacher education program. But it might not transfer with credit into an engineering program at the same university.

Most community colleges have open admissions and most four-year schools don't. Community colleges are great places to start if you have average, or below average, high school grades. You can create a solid record that'll help you get into a four-year school to complete your degree. But your classmates at a community college may not be as capable as classmates would be at a four-year school. So, take the most challenging courses available, study hard, and do <u>more</u> than required. That way, you'll be ready to succeed after you transfer. And you'll have a better chance to earn transfer scholarships.

If you plan to transfer, enroll full time at the community college, if possible. Complete your associate degree before you transfer. Go directly from the two-year to the four-year school, rather than taking time off between degrees. This way, transfer requirements won't change before you complete your studies.

If you have strong high school grades and good test scores, look into your community college's honors program. Most schools have them. They provide many benefits. (See Chapter 14 to learn more.) Also, check to see if there is a Phi Theta Kappa chapter. Phi Theta Kappa provides leadership, service, and social activities. You normally need a 3.5 or higher college GPA to join.

Phi Theta Kappa sponsors a website (collegefish.org) with tools to help transfer students. Members are eligible for special scholarships. Some are national, which work at schools across the country. Others are transfer scholarships at baccalaureate schools that target Phi Theta Kappa members. To learn more about Phi Theta Kappa, check out the group's website (ptk.org). Then talk to the Phi Theta Kappa advisor on your community college campus.

Tau Sigma is another academic honor society for transfer students. There are chapters on about 130 four-year campuses across the country. To see if there is a chapter at a school you're considering, visit tausigmanhs.org.

SUMMARY

One of the best ways to save money is to complete two years at a community college. Find one that has an articulation agreement with the school where you want to get your bachelor's degree. Meet with the transfer advisors at both schools. Pay attention to details so you complete the right courses. Take the most challenging classes available and work hard so you're ready to transfer after you earn your associate degree. To learn more about community colleges, check out websites of community colleges in your area and the American Association of Community Colleges (aacc.nche.edu).

CHAPTER 11 – START IN STATE, AND THEN TRANSFER

Have you considered starting college at an in-state public, and then transferring? You can save money by completing part of your degree at an in-state public, and then transferring to a private or out-of-state public school. For example, an Illinois student might want her degree in political science from George Washington University (GWU) in Washington, DC. She could attend University of Illinois-Springfield for two years, and then transfer to GWU to complete her bachelor's degree. In Springfield, she could focus on general education courses. She could also learn first-hand how state government works, since Springfield is the state capital. When she transferred to GWU, she could learn about federal government in the nation's capital and complete her bachelor's degree. She'd have the best of both worlds from two outstanding political science departments. The strategy would also save her about $75,000 in tuition and fees. She'd save even more if she lived at home while in Illinois.

There are advantages to completing your first two years at an in-state public. You can complete foundational classes at lower in-state rates. It's also a good strategy if you're not sure about career goals. You can use the first two years to explore careers and majors. Then you can find the best out-of-state public or private school to complete your degree.

It's also a good strategy if you don't have strong high school grades and test scores. Public schools often have lower admission standards for in-state students. You can use your time at the in-state public to build a strong academic record. You'll have a better chance for admission at the second school and maybe get transfer scholarships. You can then transfer, take specialized classes, and get your degree from the more prominent school. You also get the career placement services and alumni contacts of the more selective school.

Sounds great, doesn't it? However, it isn't common. According to the National Student Clearinghouse Research Center, only about 13 percent of those who start at four-year publics complete their degrees somewhere else. It isn't easy. And there aren't many tools to help.

Articulation agreements between four-year schools are rare. So, if you're not careful, credits won't transfer and the strategy backfires. In fact, according to the National Center for Education Statistics, students who transfer, on average, take about a year longer to graduate than students who stay at one school. So, if you want to consider this strategy, you need to understand the transfer policies of the school where you want to graduate and plan carefully. A good starting point is the school's website. Look under "prospective students" or "transfers."

Schools seldom accept more than sixty transfer credits. They also limit the number of upper-level courses that transfer. You usually have to earn a C or better grade to get transfer credit. Classes taken Pass/Fail usually won't transfer. Credits usually transfer only from regionally-accredited colleges. Most colleges and universities use *regional* accrediting agencies. For-profit colleges sometimes use *national* accrediting agencies. Just because your credits come from an accredited college doesn't mean the school has the right accreditation. Check *before* you take classes!

Most colleges and universities are picky about transfer courses matching exactly to their courses. General education (sometimes called gen ed or core) credits, which apply to many majors, are easier to transfer than more specific classes. For example, a foundational course (like English 100 or European History 201) may transfer. A more specialized class (like

Contemporary Problems of Eastern Europe 320) may not transfer, or may only transfer as an elective.

Some schools have even more rules about transfer credits. For example, many only accept recent credits. Some won't let you transfer credits in your major. Many won't transfer credit from internships (supervised work experiences).

Get an evaluation of transfer credit as early as possible. An **evaluation of course credits** tells you which credits transfer. However, most schools will only do this after you're accepted and they have your final transcript from the first school. However, by then it's too late. Ideally, you'd know what they would accept at the second school *before* you take the course at the first school.

If you're lucky, the schools you're considering already have an articulation agreement, which spells out transfer policies. Articulation agreements are common between two- and four-year schools (especially when they're in the same state). But they're rare between four-year schools that both offer baccalaureate degrees. However, there's pressure on schools to help students transfer and complete degrees. So, transferring may become easier.

If you're considering this strategy, start by looking at information for transfer students on the website of the school where you want your degree. Some schools have **Transfer Equivalency Guides** on websites. These are usually electronic databases. You can look up classes from school #1 that school #2 has reviewed. You can learn what (if any) credits have transferred. Also, look at transferology.com. Here, you can learn how specific courses from a sending (#1) school have transferred to a receiving (#2) school.

However, if you can't find transfer equivalency information on these websites, you may need to do your own matching and planning. Find out who oversees transfer credits at school #2. Seek his or her advice. The person's title might be Transfer

Coordinator or Transfer Advisor. Contact the person, and ask if they can help you transfer. Some schools will develop a tentative evaluation of course credit. However, with many schools you're on your own. If so, take the initiative and do your homework. Or find another school that has clearer transfer policies and procedures.

Even if you have a transfer agreement, get everything in writing. And save details about courses. Questions may come up later. For example, the person you work with could retire, or change jobs. Save each syllabus from courses at school #1. Save details about textbooks and readings (title, author, edition, etc.). These can be helpful if the receiving school denies credit for a course that you feel matches. The closer the course description, textbooks, and assignments, the better luck you'll have convincing decision-makers to award transfer credit.

About ten months from your transfer date, review applications and deadlines for school #2. Complete all forms (including financial aid applications). Send everything on time, to the correct address. And remember, departmental deadlines may be earlier than school deadlines.

At least six weeks before the deadline, get a copy of your official transcript from school #1. Review it. Be sure courses and grades are correct. If your name has changed, get it changed on the official transcript. If you took any courses Pass/Fail, the transcript should list the minimum passing grade. If it's a C, you may get credit. If it's a D, you probably won't. Ask the sending school to define any abbreviations or codes on your transcript.

Once it's correct, order an official copy of your transcript. Receiving schools usually won't let you send a photocopy of the transcript. Order it ahead of time, so school #2 gets it by the deadline. Be sure you have the right address. Many colleges want the transcript sent in a sealed envelope, with an official signature across the flap. If you need your transcript sent this way, let people know when you place the order.

Once the receiving school accepts you, you'll get an evaluation of course credits. It'll tell you which courses transfer. You may feel some courses that didn't get credit should. If so, gather the course syllabus, name of the textbook, copies of papers, etc. from the course. Then call and describe your situation. Ask if you can meet to discuss the classes and supporting information. Be polite and professional. The transfer advisor can be very important for your successful transfer to a new school.

If you're not successful in convincing the decision-maker, see if there is an appeal (second review) process. If so, you might want to appeal. However, you could upset someone who's also deciding on financial aid. So, be polite and professional. Don't do or say anything stupid.

If you complete more classes before you transfer, send a final transcript to get all transfer credits you deserve.

One note of caution: if you're eligible for need-based or merit-based financial aid at school #2, this strategy may not be a good one. Some schools, such as Duke University (in Durham, North Carolina), guarantee they'll meet 100 percent of admitted students' demonstrated need. Duke defines demonstrated need as "the difference between the amounts that a particular family is expected to contribute towards their student's college education and the estimated annual cost of attendance." So, if you're a low-income student, it might be less expensive to go to Duke all four years. Also, although most schools have financial aid for transfer students, it's often less than for freshmen.

If you're considering this strategy, apply as a freshman to both the in-state school and your ultimate school. Apply for both merit-based and need-based financial aid at both. This way, if both schools accept you, you can make a direct comparison of net prices. Also, look into the types and typical amounts of financial aid available for transfer students at your final school. See Chapter 27 for ideas about how to compare the net prices of attending different schools.

SUMMARY

You might save money starting at an in-state public school, and then transferring to a more expensive private or out-of-state public. But few people do it because it's difficult.

If you want to start at an in-state public and then transfer, make sure you know the transfer policies of your ultimate school. If there is no articulation agreement, look for a Transfer Equivalency Guide. Enlist the help of the person responsible for transfers at your ultimate school. And be sure to keep a copy of the syllabus from each course you want to transfer.

The good news is it's getting easier to transfer between baccalaureate schools. Everyone recognizes the barriers to transferring. Congress has held hearings about the waste this causes. With the threat of federal oversight, schools are starting to make transfers easier and more successful.

CHAPTER 12 – START (AND FINISH) AT AN IN-STATE PUBLIC

Should you get your bachelor's degree at a public university in your state? With today's college costs, many students – even wealthy ones – are attending in-state publics. Almost all students should apply to at least one in-state public university.

An in-state university could be especially attractive if you want to stay in your home state after graduation. Schools establish strong internship and job placement relationships with nearby organizations. It's also a good choice if you need to go home often. For example, you may want to stay close to a fiancé, child, or sick relative. If you plan to join a family business, a nearby college can help you stay in touch with the business or work part time.

Top students may pay the lowest net price at an in-state public. Many states offer merit-based aid for students who stay in state. Plus, publics usually offer their best school-sponsored merit aid to outstanding in-state students. For example, the University of North Carolina's Morehead-Cain Awards provide tremendous support for talented undergrads. Students can be from any income level. The awards pay for four years of tuition, housing, fees, and other expenses. They also provide a laptop computer and four years of summer experiences (often with international travel). Morehead-Cain scholars also have many leadership and enrichment opportunities. There are 50-60 new Morehead-Cain scholars each year and usually about half come from North Carolina.

Most states offer need-based scholarships and grants to students who go to school in state. Many schools also offer stronger school-sponsored need-based financial aid to in-state students.

If you are planning on graduate school, you probably need to save on your first degree. The advanced degree is usually more important for getting a well-paying job. So, an in-state public might be a great choice for your undergrad degree.

An in-state public is also a great choice if you're interested in a strong program there. For example, if you live in California and want to pursue film studies you can choose among several outstanding in-state public schools.

If you're lucky, you live in a state with an outstanding public university. Many experts argue that the Public Ivies are as good as the Ivy League. The **Public Ivies** include:

- University of Michigan
- University of Virginia
- University of California
- University of Vermont
- University of North Carolina (Chapel Hill)
- University of Texas (Austin)
- College of William and Mary
- Miami University of Ohio

There are many low-cost ways to enhance a public school education. If you choose a public, try to join the honors program. (Chapter 14 discusses honor programs.) Take part in exchanges (described in Chapter 13) and affordable international experiences (described in Chapter 42). And, get to know students from other states and countries. You can learn a lot from new friends who aren't just like your high school pals.

If you look at alumni of public universities, you'll see many famous graduates. These people all got their undergrad degrees at state schools:

- Marc Andreessen, founder of Netscape
  University of Illinois (Urbana-Champaign)
- Joe Biden, US Vice President
  University of Delaware
- Warren Buffett, CEO of Berkshire Hathaway
  University of Nebraska
- Tim Cook, CEO of Apple
  Auburn University
- Katie Couric, television personality
  University of Virginia
- Tina Fey, comedian
  University of Virginia
- Susana Martinez, governor of New Mexico
  University of Texas (El Paso)
- Doug McMillon, CEO of Walmart
  University of Arkansas
- Alan Mulally, CEO of Ford Motor Company
  University of Kansas
- Patty Murray, US Senator
  Washington State University
- Steven Spielberg, movie director and producer
  California State University (Long Beach)
- Condoleezza Rice, former US Secretary of State
  University of Denver
- Robin Roberts, television broadcaster
  Southeastern Louisiana University
- Oprah Winfrey, media CEO
  Tennessee State University

The Rhodes Scholars Program, one of the world's top graduate programs, selected many class members from public schools in 2014. They included the Universities of California (Berkeley), Tennessee, Wisconsin, and Virginia. The Rhodes program also selected graduates from Georgia Institute of Technology and Mississippi State University.

Most research shows smart, talented people who attend less-selective schools do as well in careers as similar students who attend more-selective schools. In the words of researcher Alan Krueger, "*That* you go to college is more important than *where* you go." However, researchers have found one important exception: students from poor families. Poorer students benefit from the contacts and connections at elite schools. So, if you've grown up poor, consider prestigious private universities. If you're eligible for need-based financial aid, a private school may also offer a lower net price than an in-state public. (Chapters 16 and 27 cover this.)

SUMMARY

Most students should apply to at least one in-state public school. An in-state public can be especially attractive if you might get merit aid. It can be a great choice if you need a college close to home, or if you want to stay in your home state after graduation. An in-state experience will be even better if you get to know diverse students from other states and countries. Take advantage of honors programs, exchange programs, and affordable international experiences.

CHAPTER 13 – PAY IN-STATE TUITION OUT OF STATE

Yes, you read the title correctly. There are ways to pay in-state tuition at a school in another state.

For starters – don't try to fake in-state residency. It's illegal. It's unethical. And you probably couldn't get away with it anyway. But there are times when out-of-state students can legally pay in-state tuition.

I wouldn't recommend this as a strategy, but it's important to know, if it fits. When divorced parents with joint custody live in different states, public schools in both states may offer in-state tuition. If you apply as a resident in a state where you didn't go to high school, you'll probably need to provide copies of custody agreements and financial support records.

RECIPROCITY AGREEMENTS

Even if you've lived with both parents and in one state your whole life, you may qualify for in-state tuition (or slightly more) in another state. Some states have **reciprocity agreements** with neighboring states. Students attend college in either state, yet pay in-state tuition. Since these are usually tuition cuts, rather than grants or scholarships, students are still eligible for a full range of financial aid.

For example, if you live in Wisconsin you can attend Minnesota publics for about the same price you'd pay in Wisconsin. Students can apply at heab.wi.gov/reciprocity. Minnesota students also pay reduced rates at Wisconsin publics. Minnesota students can get more information at their state higher education website, ohe.state.mn.us.

Students in fifteen Western states get tuition discounts at publics in the other states. These states are:

- Alaska
- Arizona
- California
- Colorado
- Hawaii
- Idaho
- Montana
- Nevada
- New Mexico
- North Dakota
- Oregon
- South Dakota
- Utah
- Washington
- Wyoming

Students typically pay 150 percent of resident tuition. For more information, check the Western Interstate Commission for Higher Education (WICHE) website at wiche.edu. Search "student exchange program."

Students in nine Midwestern states (Illinois, Indiana, Kansas, Michigan, Minnesota, Missouri, Nebraska, North Dakota, and Wisconsin) can pay lower tuition at some out-of-state schools. Through the Midwest Student Exchange Program (MSEP), public schools charge students no more than 150 percent of in-state tuition for some majors. Private schools also offer discounts. To learn more, visit the MSEP website at msep.mhec.org.

Students who live in Southern Regional Education Board (SREB) states can attend college in other SREB states at in-state rates if the major they want isn't available in their home state. SREB states aren't just in the South. SREB states include:

- Alabama
- Arkansas
- Delaware
- Florida
- Georgia
- Kentucky
- Louisiana
- Maryland
- Mississippi
- North Carolina
- Oklahoma
- South Carolina
- Tennessee
- Texas
- Virginia
- West Virginia

SREB calls this program the Academic Common Market. To learn more, visit sreb.org.

New England's Tuition Break gives breaks to residents of Connecticut, Maine, Massachusetts, New Hampshire, Rhode Island, and Vermont. Students get the break when they study majors that aren't available at publics in their home states. For more information, visit the New England Board of Higher Education website at nebhe.org.

Your high school counselor probably knows about agreements in your state. Or you can get information about reciprocal agreements from your state department or commission of higher education. The US Department of Education website lists the websites and contact information for these. Search "state contacts" at ed.gov.

DISTRICT OF COLUMBIA TUITION ASSISTANCE GRANT

If you live in the District of Columbia, you're eligible for an even better deal. It's the District of Columbia Tuition Assistance Grant (DC TAG). You must be a US citizen no older than 24 and live in DC for a year before college. You can go to any US public college or university. DC TAG pays the difference between in-state and out-of-state tuition up to $10,000 each year. There is a lifetime cap of $50,000. Alternatively, DC TAG will pay up to $2500 per year toward tuition at private schools in the District. DC TAG will also pay up to $2500 per year toward tuition at a two-year college anywhere in the country. Students can renew these $2500 grants each year for up to five years. To find out more about DC TAG, visit the DC Superintendent of Education website (osse.dc.gov/service/dc-tuition-assistance-grant-dc-tag). The District also has the DC College Access Program (DC CAP), a privately-funded program. It provides college counseling and financial aid to students in the District.

EXCHANGE PROGRAMS

Another way to study out of state at in-state rates is an exchange program. There are many exchanges between individual colleges. There is also a national program known as the National Student Exchange (nse.org). About 3500 students from nearly 200 schools (including some in Canada, Guam, Puerto Rico, and the US Virgin Islands), take part each year. Exchanges last up to one year. Students usually pay normal tuition and fees at their home school. Sometimes they pay in-state tuition at the host school. They pay room and board fees (which don't vary much among schools) to the host school. Students apply for financial aid from their home schools. Coordinators on each campus help students work through details and make sure credits transfer.

These exchanges offer ways to take courses that aren't available on your home campus. Or you can explore new fields while living in a different part of North America. For example, an education major at the University of Utah might spend a semester at Queen's College in New York. In New York, he'd live in one of our nation's most ethnically diverse areas. Or a student studying animal science at Iowa State University could take marine biology classes at Florida International University. Students at landlocked Iowa State wouldn't have many other opportunities to observe whales, dolphins, and manatees!

Exchanges provide a way to learn from leading professors in your field. If you're thinking about a graduate degree, it's also a great way to learn about the school you're considering. You can meet and work with professors there. Sometimes you can even conduct research during a yearlong exchange. What a fantastic way to get an inside track on graduate school admissions and financial aid! For more information about the National Student Exchange, check nse.org.

ESTABLISH RESIDENCY

Another way to pay in-state fees at an out-of-state school is to move to the state. This may make sense for an out-of-state school with much lower in-state rates. And it might be a great strategy if you take time off between high school and college. Most states won't consider you a resident if you move to the state *just* to go to school. Normally, you must live there full time for at least one year to qualify for in-state tuition. In some states, the requirement is a full year before you apply. In others, it's a full year before you start classes. College websites usually explain residency requirements. Type "residency" or "(state name) residency" into the search engine. You can also check the state's department of higher education website. Or you can send your questions to the admissions office.

You usually need to move to the state and get an apartment, job, and driver's license. You also need to vote and file income taxes there. State laws control residency, so requirements vary state to state. Schools enforce residency requirements strictly. So, study requirements *before* you apply.

GET OUT-OF-STATE TUITION WAIVED

Many schools provide out-of-state tuition waivers in financial aid packages. If you have high ACT or SAT test scores and a strong high school GPA, ask the admissions office about out-of-state tuition waivers.

Many schools waive out-of-state tuition for military veterans. Some waive out-of-state tuition for military spouses and dependents, too. Check to see if the school has a website dedicated to student-veterans. If not, contact the admissions office and ask if the school waives out-of-state tuition for veterans.

SUMMARY

There are ways to pay in-state tuition at a public school in another state. Some states have reciprocity agreements with neighboring states. Exchange programs also let students pay in-state tuition. And you can qualify for in-state tuition by setting up residency in a state one year before you start college.

If you're a top student, you may get out-of-state tuition waived. Military veterans, spouses, and dependents may also qualify for out-of-state tuition waivers. If you can make it happen, you can save tens of thousands of dollars.

CHAPTER 14 – BECOME AN HONORS OR CO-OP STUDENT

Have you thought about honors or co-op programs? These offer outstanding affordable education experiences.

HONORS PROGRAMS

If you join an honors program at an in-state public, you'll get a top-notch education at a bargain price. Out-of-state programs can also be great values if you get scholarships, grants, or an out-of-state tuition waiver. And remember, honors programs aren't just at four-year schools. Many community colleges have fantastic honors programs, too. (See the section about honors programs and Phi Kappa Phi in Chapter 10.)

Honors classes are often seminars taught by top professors. A **seminar** is a series of small group sessions where everyone participates. Talented students challenge and learn from each another, as well as from professors.

Honors students have better chances for scholarships than other students do. For example, they often get study-abroad scholarships. Many schools pay honor student expenses to attend conferences and special events.

Another advantage is flexibility. Colleges have many rules. But honors students sometimes get to break them. For example, honors students often get required courses waived. Sometimes they can take similar classes that are more interesting or challenging. Honors students at some schools can even create individualized majors.

Honors students usually get top-notch career and academic advising. Some schools offer leadership training and experiences. Honors programs can also prepare you for graduate school. You can do undergrad research and projects with professors. Honors programs also help students apply for and get funding for graduate school.

Students in honors programs often get low-cost or free admission to lectures, concerts, plays, and art exhibits. They have lunches and dinners with faculty. It's a great way to experience exciting cultural events without having to spend much money.

Honors students also sometimes get opportunities to tutor other students – for pay. Tutoring is a good way to decide if you enjoy teaching. And if you earn money, it's a bonus! Juniors and seniors in honors programs may even qualify for paid teaching or research assistantships. (Read Chapter 31 for more information.)

Most colleges and universities let honors students register early. So, you get the classes you need and your choice of class times. Honors students also sometimes get special study rooms, libraries, and computer labs. At some schools honors students can also live in special dorms with other serious students. Some schools even hold classes and have faculty offices in honors dorms.

Many honors programs participate in the National Student Exchange (NSE) discussed in the last chapter. Students can study at another university for up to one year. Honors semesters through the National Collegiate Honors Council (NCHC) also allow students to study away from their home campuses. They combine field studies, research, and seminars with evening and weekend social and educational experiences. For more information, visit nchchonors.org.

Babson College provides an outstanding undergraduate business education for all students. Student teams start real businesses. Babson honors students can complete international experiences like overseas internships or courses at the London School of Economics.

Besides its honors program, the University of North Carolina (UNC) at Chapel Hill has two outstanding programs, the Morehead-Cain Scholars and the Robertson Scholars. Morehead-Cain Scholars get free tuition, room, board, and books. The scholars also get a free laptop, summer internships, and international travel opportunities. It doesn't get much better than that – unless you're a Robertson Scholar. In this program, half of the students are from UNC and half are from Duke University in nearby Durham. Students study at both universities. The Robertson program also includes summer enrichment activities. Students receive money each summer to pay for transportation, living expenses, and materials.

Western Washington University, in Bellingham, has a traditional honors program and Fairhaven College. Fairhaven sometimes accepts students who *don't* have strong academic records. Students learn in a cooperative, rather than a competitive, atmosphere. Fairhaven has a well-known Law, Diversity, and Justice Program.

So, how do you join an honors program? If you're an A or B+ high school student and have strong test scores, you'll likely qualify. Check school websites to learn details. Search "honors" at the schools you're considering. You may need to apply to honors programs when you apply to colleges. Some schools invite students based on high school grades and test scores. Others invite students after they enroll based on college grades and recommendations. If you are invited, say yes!

I got an invitation to join the honors program when I was an undergrad. I didn't know anyone else in the honors program, and I didn't really understand what it was. Plus, I somehow thought it would cost more money, which I didn't have. So, I said no. I regret that decision. I passed up a great opportunity. Don't make the same mistake. If you have a chance to join an honors program, do it!

CO-OP PROGRAMS

Cooperative education programs make college relevant *and* affordable. In **cooperative education** (sometimes called **co-op, work-integrated education,** or **experience-based education**), students alternate between working and studying. Programs vary from college to college (and even between departments within a college).

Students begin co-op programs after at least two semesters of full-time college. In an **alternating program**, you work around forty hours each week and don't take any college classes. In a **parallel program**, you work about twenty hours each week and go to school part time. Parallel programs are less common since they usually have to be in the same location as the college. Many bachelor's degree co-op programs take five years to complete. (Some community colleges offer programs that work similarly to co-op programs. In community colleges, these are sometimes apprenticeship programs.)

Co-op programs are most common in engineering and industrial fields. However, they're available for many college majors. You normally stay with the same organization (usually in different jobs or divisions) throughout college. Multinational corporations, non-profit agencies, and government offices participate. A co-op program with a multinational company may even include a rotation in a country outside the US. The wages you earn depend on your field of study, your prior work experience, your education or training, the organization, and the job market.

A co-op is a great way to explore careers and get experience. You build your resume and make professional contacts. You gain experience in applying and interviewing for jobs, setting and meeting goals, and working in teams. A strong co-op program gives you on-the-job experiences that expand your knowledge and reinforce your classroom studies. You apply theory and facts to solve real problems.

Drexel University, based in Philadelphia, has one of the country's strongest co-op programs. Students go to school full time the first year. Then they rotate between six months of school and six months of paid employment with one of about 1600 co-op partners. These include corporations, non-profits, and government agencies. Drexel has co-op partners in most states and in about 50 international locations.

Sometimes co-op programs include scholarships or grants. For example, eleven universities join with WACE for the National Co-op Scholarship program. The schools are:

- Clarkson University

- Drexel University

- Johnson & Wales University

- Kettering University

- Merrimack College

- Rochester Institute for Technology

- State University of New York (Oswego)

- University of Cincinnati

- University of Massachusetts (Lowell)

- University of Toledo

- Wentworth Institute of Technology

Each year the program provides nearly 200 merit-based scholarships, worth about $5 million, to high school and transfer students who want to be involved in cooperative education at one of these schools. For more information, visit waceinc.org.

Many employers hire students from their co-op programs. If you go with the company, you often receive work credit for the co-op experience. So, you start out at a higher salary and with more vacation and other benefits.

I'm a strong believer in co-op programs. My husband completed a four-year co-op with FMC Corporation and went with FMC when he graduated. His co-op rotations were at an FMC facility in his hometown, so he was able to live with his parents and save money. He made enough during each co-op rotation to pay for the next school term. When he graduated, FMC offered him a job with two years of work credit, vacation credit, and a fantastic starting salary. Plus, FMC was his first choice among potential employers.

To find schools that offer co-op programs, check the directory at the Cooperative Education and Internship Association (ceiainc.org). For more information about individual school programs, search "cooperative education" on college and departmental websites.

SUMMARY

Honors and cooperative education programs are great ways to get an extraordinary education at an affordable cost.

If you want the most out of college, put honors programs high on your list of possibilities. Honors programs at public colleges and universities have many of the qualities of a small, private, liberal arts college. To learn about individual honors programs check the websites of specific schools.

Strong cooperative education programs let you apply classroom learning to on-the-job situations. A well-paying experience can also help pay for college, especially if you can live inexpensively during your co-op rotations. These experiences build your resume and usually lead to better job offers when you graduate.

CHAPTER 15 – CHECK OUT LOW-COST PRIVATE SCHOOLS

Would you believe it if someone said you could get a private liberal arts degree and graduate with a job – with <u>no</u> student loan debt? It's possible. Keep reading.

The sticker price of a private (independent) school is typically more than a similar public. However, there are wide ranges in private school costs. In fact, a few US privates charge little or no tuition. A few US privates offer four-year degrees at very low cost to students.

BEREA COLLEGE AND ALICE LLOYD COLLEGE

Berea College and Alice Lloyd College, both in Kentucky, serve low-income students with strong academic potential. Many come from Appalachia. Students carry a full course load. But they also work part time at on-campus or community jobs. Jobs usually relate to the student's career plans. Some students also work on campus during summer. Graduates of both schools praise the work and career exploration opportunities. Employers value the work ethic, self-reliance, and skills of Berea and Alice Lloyd graduates. Students usually graduate debt free and with jobs. To learn more about these schools, visit their websites (berea.edu and alc.edu).

COLLEGE OF THE OZARKS

College of the Ozarks, in Missouri, is similar. Nicknamed "Hard Work U," College of the Ozarks also targets low-income students. Each student works fifteen hours per week in one of eighty career areas. Agriculture, computers, food service, and construction are some of the areas. Some students earn extra income working part time in nearby Hollister or Branson, Missouri. Students also work two forty-hour weeks during summer or another break. The college discourages student debt and doesn't even offer student loans. However, most students graduate debt free. College of the Ozarks regularly ranks among the best small liberal arts schools in the country. To learn more about College of the Ozarks, visit cofo.edu.

THE WEBB INSTITUTE

If you're interested in naval architecture and marine engineering, the Webb Institute provides a great low-cost opportunity. It's a small, top-ranked school. About eighty students live on the 26-acre campus on the beach in Long Island, New York. They study ship design and systems, plus marine, electrical, and mechanical engineering. They also study civil and structural engineering. Students get to know other students and teachers well, since there are just ten full-time faculty members who teach at Webb. The school offers a full-tuition scholarship for every student. Students pay for their room, board, books, laptop computer, transportation, and personal expenses (about $20,000 total per year). Other need-based scholarships are available. Students can also apply for federal grants and outside scholarships to reduce expenses. And students earn money during work rotations.

During the two-month winter term, Webb students work in the maritime industry in various places around the world. And students all spend time at sea. It's much like an internship program (see Chapter 41). Students see the practical side of their studies and apply theories they've learned in classes. They earn money. And they graduate with at least eight months of relevant work experience. It's one reason Webb has an incredible job placement record. So, if you're physically fit and know marine engineering or naval architecture is the profession for you, check out the Webb Institute (webb.edu).

DEEP SPRINGS COLLEGE

If you're a studious guy, love the outdoors, and always dreamed of being a cowboy, Deep Springs College could be the answer to your prayers. It's a two-year liberal arts school with just 26 students – all male. It's on a 120-square mile cattle ranch and alfalfa farm in California. In exchange for working as a ranch hand at least twenty hours a week, students get free room, board, and tuition. Students pay about $3000 each year for travel, books, and incidentals. Students get an intense, interactive learning experience in their two years at Deep Springs. Deep Springs accepts only serious students. They decide the subjects they'll study and develop goals for each class. There are just two mandatory subjects: composition and public speaking.

Deep Springs' faculty members live on site. So, students interact with their teachers in and out of class. Students develop self-discipline, self-reliance, and responsibility. They have opportunities to be leaders *and* followers. Deep Springs awards associate degrees. Graduates have gone on to complete bachelor's degrees at many Ivy League and other top universities. Deep Springs offers a unique, unconventional, and affordable start to college. To learn more, visit deepsprings.edu.

BRIGHAM YOUNG UNIVERSITY

If you're a Mormon, consider Brigham Young University (BYU) in Provo, Utah. The school is highly ranked. And it offers tremendous value. The Church of Jesus Christ of Latter-day Saints (LDS) founded BYU. The church continues to provide guidance and financial support. The school strives to develop students spiritually, as well as intellectually. The church guides activities both in and out of the classroom. So, things like excessive drinking that you see on many campuses don't happen at BYU. Students also adhere to a strict honor code.

Tuition at BYU is only about $10,000 per year for non-LDS students – and about half that for members of the church. Plus, the school offers generous need-, talent- and merit-based financial aid. Combine that with a broad range of majors and outstanding advising, and you get a very high-value college education. Learn more at byu.edu.

SUMMARY

It's possible to get a private liberal arts education almost free! However, Berea, Alice Lloyd, Deep Springs, Webb, and College of the Ozarks together have fewer than 3300 students. And it's tough to get in.

Brigham Young University is much larger. There are about 25,000 full-time undergraduates. And, BYU admits about half of their applicants. So, you'd have a better chance of being accepted. Learn more at byu.edu.

These schools aren't for everyone – and they don't try to be. But if they sound like a good match for your interests and values, find out more and apply. These schools offer a range of high-quality educational, spiritual, character, and career development experiences – at prices that are hard to beat!

CHAPTER 16 – CONSIDER OTHER HIGH-VALUE PRIVATE SCHOOLS

Other private colleges and universities are too expensive to consider, right? Wrong!

Lower- and middle-income students often apply only to community colleges and in-state publics. They don't consider private (independent) schools, because they don't think they can afford them. Don't make that mistake. Ignore the sticker price and apply to the best schools where you meet the qualifications.

During the past decade, state leaders had to make tough financial choices. State schools raised tuition and fees – often dramatically. Private schools didn't raise them as much. So, the price difference shrank. With financial aid, a private may even offer you a <u>lower</u> net price than a public – especially if you qualify for both merit- and need-based aid, or if you'd help make the school more diverse.

Private schools also have better records for graduating students, and graduating them in less time. The fewer semesters you have to pay tuition, fees, room, and board, the more affordable a school becomes. So, give private schools some thought.

LOOK FOR NEED-BLIND ADMISSIONS AND 100 PERCENT FUNDING OF INSTITUTIONALLY-DETERMINED NEED

Many privates have large amounts of money called **endowments**. Endowments exist when **alumni** (graduates of the school) and others contribute for future needs. The school invests the money. Investment income then pays for scholarships, new buildings, or other projects identified by donors. For example, Grinnell College, a small liberal arts school in Iowa with about 1600 students, has a 1.6 billion dollar endowment. Some of that money funds student scholarships. So, Grinnell admits qualified students without considering their ability to pay. Grinnell might determine your family cannot afford to pay much for college. If so, they make up the rest with financial aid. Nine out of every ten Grinnell students receive financial aid.

Princeton University is another top-rated school with a high sticker price and low net price for qualified low- and middle-income students. The sticker price for one year at Princeton is more than $60,000. However, Princeton has need-blind admissions. And Princeton guarantees that it'll provide 100 percent of the institutionally-defined need. About 60 percent of students get financial aid.

So, if you're a lower- or middle-income student, look for colleges like Grinnell and Princeton – schools that have need-blind admissions. And, look for colleges that will fund 100 percent of the institutionally-determined need. The **institutionally-determined need** is the difference between the total price of attending the school and the amount the school thinks your family can afford to pay. Colleges decide the amount based on the information you submit on the FAFSA, PROFILE, or other financial aid forms. However, there aren't many of these schools. In fact, there are only about sixty of them in the entire United States.

Read the *US News* annual ranking of the best values in colleges. The print version of the guide is often at libraries and in high school guidance offices. Some of the information is also available free at usnews.com. *US News* bases its ranking on a school's quality compared with the net price of attending (for a student who receives the average financial aid package). Colleges that provide high levels of financial aid compared to the cost of attending rank high on the value index.

Kiplinger's Personal Finance develops and publishes a similar ranking of the best values in private schools. Search "best college values" at kiplinger.com. Learn about schools that have need-blind admissions and fund 100 percent of institutionally-determined need. If it looks like you'll meet admission standards and you're a low- or middle- income student, give these private schools a chance.

If you're a highly-qualified low-income student, check out QuestBridge (questbridge.org). QuestBridge provides an internet-based meeting point. It links exceptional students with colleges, scholarship providers, and enrichment programs. QuestBridge's College Prep Scholarship helps outstanding low-income high school juniors prepare for college applications. Their National College Match helps outstanding low-income high school seniors gain admission and scholarships to 35 selective (mostly private) colleges.

If you're a highly-qualified student who *won't* qualify for need-based aid, you should still consider private schools. You might get a great net price with merit-based aid. You'll get better merit offers if your test scores and GPA are higher than average. You can find average ACT scores, SAT scores, and GPAs for enrolled students on each school's website.

SOME PRIVATES GIVE SCHOLARSHIPS TO ALL STUDENTS

Some outstanding private schools offer scholarships to all admitted students. An example is Olin, in Massachusetts, a unique engineering college that opened in 2002. All Olin students receive a half-tuition scholarship for all four years of undergraduate study without regard to their financial situation. Students pay for half of their tuition, plus housing, food, a laptop computer, books, supplies, and miscellaneous expenses. Admission is need-blind. Need-based grants are available from Olin and the college tries to meet the student's full, demonstrated financial need. So, if you're a creative math and science whiz who's interested in a unique engineering education, check out Olin's website (olin.edu).

OTHER OPPORTUNITIES

Many schools affiliated (connected) with churches provide high-quality, affordable private education. Members of the church often get lower tuition. Many schools have scholarships for members, too.

You may also find good value at a private school if you transfer. For example, if your community college has an articulation agreement with the school and you have a strong record, you may get scholarships and grants. Some top-ranked private colleges (including Amherst, Bates, Bucknell, Mount Holyoke, Harvard, Bryn Mawr, Stanford, Wellesley, Vassar, and Smith) actively recruit top community college transfers. Some of these schools have both need-blind admissions policies and fund 100 percent of demonstrated need.

SUMMARY

Give private colleges and universities a chance to provide a high quality, affordable education. Look beyond the sticker price, particularly if you're a top low- or middle-income student. Give them a chance to make you an offer you can't refuse!

CHAPTER 17 – TAKE ADVANTAGE OF FAMILY CONNECTIONS

Do you have family connections that can lead to college discounts?

Many schools offer discounts if you have a parent, grandparent, spouse, brother, or sister connected to the school. These discounts range from a few hundred dollars to full four-year tuition. So, learn about and take advantage of family discounts.

You're a **legacy** student if you attend a school where a parent or grandparent graduated. And you might qualify for a discount. Tuition discounts for children of graduates are most common at private colleges and universities. For example, Luther College in Decorah, Iowa, offers a Luther Legacy Award, $1000 each year for four years, to full-time students whose parent graduated from Luther. Dominican University (near Chicago) provides legacy awards of $2000 each year for up to four years. Hood College (in Frederick, Maryland) gives Heritage Scholarships, $1000 per year for up to four years, to students who have a parent or grandparent who graduated from Hood. Legacy discounts are less common at public schools. But some, like the University of Iowa, offer legacy discounts and special legacy scholarship opportunities.

Some schools offer discounts to families with more than one child enrolled. For example, George Washington University (GWU), in DC, offers a Family Grant. It pays half tuition for full-time undergraduates with a **sibling** (brother or sister) attending as a full-time undergraduate at the same time. And at GWU, with tuition close to $50,000 per year, that means big savings!

Is your mother or father a college faculty or staff member? If so, you may get huge discounts for college. Many private schools (and some publics) waive tuition for children (and sometimes spouses) of employees.

Some schools have **reciprocal** (two-way) arrangements with other schools. For example, Stephens College (in Columbia, Missouri) waives tuition for up to eight semesters of full-time study for students with a parent on the faculty or staff. And Stephens takes part in two tuition reciprocity programs. So, students get free or reduced-tuition at other schools, too. The Council of Independent Colleges has about 400 member schools. The Tuition Exchange has about 600 member schools. Therefore, students with a parent who works at Stephens College can attend college at a huge range of colleges and universities – and pay little or no tuition. If you have a parent who works at a college, check with the human resources department to see if the school takes part in tuition exchange programs.

Family connections are also important for scholarships. If your parent is a minister, firefighter, union member, police officer, teacher, or military veteran, you have scholarship opportunities. (See Chapter 25 for more information.)

Summary

Family connections can sometimes mean discounts for college. Your best discounts are through colleges where a parent works, a parent graduated, or a sibling studies.

CHAPTER 18 – GET A DEGREE OUTSIDE THE US

Have you ever thought about studying outside the United States? There are both fun and practical reasons to consider it. One of the best times to live abroad is when you're young, without a house or family responsibilities. As organizations become more multinational and global, it can help you land a good job and advance in your career.

One way to experience international education is to study outside the United States for your whole degree. It sounds expensive, but it can be affordable. If you're a **full-pay student** (you don't qualify for financial aid), it may even be *less* expensive to get a degree outside the US.

CANADA, THE UNITED KINGDOM, AND AUSTRALIA

The most popular places to study outside the US are Canada, the United Kingdom (UK), and Australia. Students study in English, yet experience another culture. Plus, you can often earn an undergraduate degree in three years. You complete a fourth year for an honors degree. (Graduate schools usually require them.) Some professional degrees, such as engineering, take five years. (Some US schools also offer three-year bachelor's degrees. See Chapter 9 for more information.)

Degrees from universities in Canada, the UK, or Australia are similar to American degrees. There is little financial aid for international students. But with the right visa, you can work part time. Part-time work provides money and it provides great experience if you're planning a career in international business or foreign relations. Many US companies recruit on Canadian campuses. Visit topuniversities.com to learn more.

Canada has community colleges, small liberal arts colleges, and major research universities. There are both public and private schools. Many US citizens attend McGill University in Montreal. It's an English-language university. But it's located in one of the world's largest French-language cities. For information about attending college in Canada, check studyincanada.com. *Maclean's*, a Canadian magazine, has a website about Canadian colleges and universities (oncampus.macleans.ca/education).

Studying in the UK offers benefits like Canada. Plus, students can easily travel to Europe and Scandinavia. To find out about studying in the UK, check ucas.com. This is the site for the Universities and Colleges Admissions Service (UCAS). Also, check educationuk.org, a British Council site where you can search for specific courses of study. Also, check timeshighereducation.co.uk, the *Times Higher Education* website.

Australia offers similar benefits. Classes are in English and undergrad degrees take three years. Australian universities begin in March and run until December. All Australian universities (sometimes called **uni's**) accept international students. Most are public and they offer affordable education. However, if you want to come home often, your savings may disappear. Airfare between the US and Australia is very expensive. To learn more, check out studyinaustralia.gov.au.

GERMANY

German public colleges and universities offer free tuition for all students – including foreigners. Some (but not all) German colleges teach classes in English. That's because English is the international language in business and Germany wants its students to be able to communicate in English. Students in Germany also get many discounts, including free or low-cost transportation. Learn more at studying-in-germany.org and daad.de/en.

SPAIN

The US needs more teachers, doctors, nurses, lawyers, and communicators who are bilingual in English and Spanish. If you understand Spanish, consider studying in Spain. Spain has good liberal arts universities that recruit international students. They promote Spain as a lower-cost option for Hispanics and other Spanish-speaking students. However, you should remember there are many dialects (language variations) in Spain. European Spanish and Spanish of the Americas are somewhat different. To learn more, check out studyinspain.info, spainedu.org, and studyineurope.eu.

OTHER COUNTRIES

US students study in many other countries around the world for bachelor's degrees. The website of the National Association of College Admissions Counselors (nacacnet.org) is a good place to begin learning about those opportunities. The site includes links to college sites in Canada, the UK, Australia, Spain, and Germany, plus many other countries.

FINANCIAL AID AND WORK OPPORTUNITIES

There are few scholarships or grants (called **bursaries** in many other countries) for international students. If you're eligible for financial aid, the net price of attending a school outside the United States will likely be higher than in the US. US federal student loans apply at some, but not all, foreign colleges and universities. The US Department of Education has a section on its website (studentaid.ed.gov) that details the types of financial aid available to study for a full degree outside the US and the procedures for applying for federal aid.

There may be opportunities to work while studying abroad. It's a great experience, especially for those interested in international business or international relations. However, international students must get employment authorization (usually called a **work visa**) from the host country's government.

OTHER ISSUES

Studying at a foreign university takes planning. Admissions take longer than in the US. So, allow extra time. You will need a current passport and **student visa** (sometimes called a **study permit** or **student authorization**). You can get a passport at any time. However, you need a college letter of acceptance before applying for a student visa. You must also get travel and housing arrangements made well ahead of the college start date. You may also need to send medical records and proof of health insurance coverage. Other countries' national health insurance usually doesn't cover international students.

Students who study outside the US must consider **monetary exchange rates** (the worth of the US dollar compared to the worth of the host country's money). The relative worth of currencies varies each day.

If you're unsure of your college major, studying for a three-year degree might not be a good choice. Most US students take general education courses for the first two years of study, and then take classes in their major. In most three-year degrees, students focus on their area of specialty from the first year of study. So, it's hard to switch majors. It can even mean starting over. If you're unsure of your major, you're better off studying in the US and doing an international exchange. (See Chapter 42 for more information.)

SUMMARY

Consider earning your degree outside the United States. The most popular places are Canada, the United Kingdom, and Australia. You take classes in English and it may take just three years to earn your degree. Spain offers an affordable choice for students fluent in Spanish. Depending on your major, your comfort living far from home, currency exchange rates, and the safety of international travel, it could be a great way to get an affordable, world-class education.

CHAPTER 19 – LET THE MILITARY PAY

Are you interested in a military career? The US Army, Air Force, Marines, Navy, and Coast Guard all provide education opportunities before, during, and after military service.

MILITARY ACADEMIES

If you have outstanding high school grades, leadership, and activities (and you're physically fit), you may want to apply to a military academy:

- US Military Academy (Army)
  West Point, New York
- US Naval Academy (Navy and Marines)
  Annapolis, Maryland
- US Air Force Academy
  Colorado Springs, Colorado
- US Coast Guard Academy
  New London, Connecticut
- US Merchant Marine Academy
  Kings Point, New York

These offer strong academics, plus military and leadership training. All students get full four-year scholarships, including tuition, books, room, and board, plus free medical and dental care. Students earn undergrad degrees at almost no cost. After graduation, they become officers and begin active duty.

Academy **appointments** (selections) are extremely competitive. If you want to attend a military academy, start the appointment/application process early. It begins much earlier than other college applications – by the beginning of you junior year in high school.

To learn about the US military academies, visit:

- Cga.edu (US Coast Guard Academy)
- Usma.edu (US Military Academy)
- Usna.edu (US Naval Academy)
- Usafa.edu (US Air Force Academy)
- Usmma.edu (US Merchant Marine Academy)

RESERVE OFFICERS' TRAINING CORPS

If you're interested in becoming an officer, consider the Reserve Officers' Training Corps (ROTC). It provides some of the same benefits as a military academy and it's easier to be accepted. ROTC is a college-based program to train officers for the armed forces. Students take part in classes and drills during the school year and summers. The US Coast Guard's College Student Pre-commissioning Initiative (CSPI) is similar.

You can participate in ROTC even if you haven't decided to join the military. ROTC provides excellent physical and leadership training. Students learn to place group goals above their own, to accept orders, and to carry them out. If you want to serve in the military after college, you can apply for a two-, three- or four-year ROTC scholarship. These pay tuition and fees. Some pay housing allowances, too. ROTC scholarships only consider merit. So, whether your family is rich or poor, you can earn one. You can also earn extra money if you study the language of Iraq, Afghanistan, China, or another region critical to national security.

When you accept an ROTC scholarship, complete the program, and graduate, you then receive more training and become an officer. Your **service commitment** (amount of time you must serve) depends on your scholarships and other factors. Most people serve two years in active service for every year they receive scholarships. Some serve in the Reserves or National Guard rather than on active duty. ROTC graduates are eligible for additional education benefits during and after their service. Many earn graduate or professional degrees.

Search "ROTC" on websites of colleges you're considering. The Army, Navy/Marines, and Air Force ROTC websites (armyrotc.com, nrotc.navy.mil, and afrotc.com) list ROTC schools. The Coast Guard website (gocoastguard.com/cspi) lists College Student Pre-commissioning Initiative schools.

Senior Military Colleges (SMCs) have some of the strongest ROTC programs. The **Corps of Cadets** (students in ROTC) often wear uniforms on campus. At the Citadel (in Charleston, South Carolina), all undergrads are cadets. Virginia Women's Institute for Leadership, at Mary Baldwin College in Staunton, is an all-female cadet corps. Other SMCs are Texas A & M University (College Station), University of North Georgia (Dahlonega), Virginia Military Institute (Lexington), Virginia Polytechnic Institute (Blacksburg) and Norwich University (Northfield, Vermont).

There are also **Military Junior Colleges**. These are two- rather than four-year programs. Students take part in ROTC's **Early Commissioning Program** (ECP). Students graduate with an associate degree and a **commission** (appointment) as an officer, an Army Second Lieutenant. They can then finish their bachelor's degrees with military support. The Military Junior Colleges are Wentworth Military College (Lexington, Missouri), Valley Forge Military College (Wayne, Pennsylvania), New Mexico Military Institute (Roswell, New Mexico), Marion Military Institute (Marion, Alabama), and Georgia Military College (Milledgeville, Georgia).

NATIONAL GUARD AND RESERVES

You can also serve and get college support through the **National Guard** and **Reserves**. We need people who are trained and ready to serve in case there is a war or other national emergency. In an emergency, these people move into active duty. The Army, Navy, Marines, Air Force, and Coast Guard each have **reserve** (backup) units. There are also Air and Army National Guard units. These units can be **called up** (activated) for national emergencies. Governors can also call up National Guard units in their states for state emergencies.

National Guard members train like new military recruits. After **basic training** (initial entry training), they complete advanced training. They learn special skills needed for their Guard jobs. Guard members then train one weekend each month and two weeks each summer. Training schedules try to avoid college conflicts.

If you join the National Guard, you get a monthly **stipend** (allowance) and **tuition reimbursement** (repayment). You also get affordable healthcare and life insurance. Many states provide extra financial aid to members of the Guard. Members may get all expenses paid at in-state publics. The risk, of course, is being called into active duty. Some short-term assignments, like helping during natural disasters, are inconvenient. But a longer-term call up can disrupt – or end – education plans. For more information visit www.arng.army.mil (Army National Guard) and www.goang.com (Air National Guard), or talk with your local National Guard recruiter. Military benefits for people in the Reserves (**Reservists**) are similar. However, most states do not offer extra college benefits for Reservists. Learn about the Reserves at:

- Goarmy.com
- Gocoastguard.com
- Marines.com
- Navy.com
- Airforce.com
- Todaysmilitary.com

EDUCATION BENEFITS FOR ENLISTED PERSONNEL

The Army, Navy, and Air Force have loan repayment programs that help **enlisted** (non-officer) personnel pay off college loans. So, after you graduate college, a military recruiter may offer you loan repayment programs as an incentive to **enlist** (join). These programs have many different processes, requirements, and benefits.

The military also has education benefits for people who enlist right out of high school. You join for a set **enlistment term** (length of time). After basic training, you train for your **military assignment** (job). This training may be like community college classes. You can sometimes get college credit for it (see Chapter 8). Other training is similar to technical or community college certificate programs. You usually can't earn college credit for this training.

You can also take college courses during off hours. The easiest way to study is at a school that offers degrees online. (Read Chapter 22.) People in the military usually don't live in one place long enough to get a traditional degree. You can take distance classes, even on Navy ships or submarines. Servicemembers can get information about tuition aid from their service representative or at military.com.

EDUCATION BENEFITS FOR MILITARY VETERANS

Veterans (former service members) can also get GI education benefits. (**GI** stands for **government issued**. For example, military uniforms are government issued. Some people call military service members "GIs.") GI Bills provide different benefits. Sometimes you must put part of your pay into an education fund that you can use later. The Department of Veteran's Affairs suggests new enlistees sign up. If you join, the government takes a small amount from your pay each month during your first year of service. In return, you get education benefits for college after you serve. You get up to 100 percent of in-state tuition and fees, plus allowances for housing and books. Benefits pay for up to 36 academic months (four years of college). Recruiters may offer other special deals to meet recruiting goals. Benefit amounts and requirements vary. Learn about these opportunities at the same sights as those listed for the Reserves, on the previous page.

Most public colleges and universities offer in-state tuition for all veterans, so you can use benefits at public schools outside your home state. Some schools extend in-state tuition benefits to spouses and dependents, too. Many privates also take part in the GI Bill Yellow Ribbon program. It provides tuition benefits that can make private schools as affordable as in-state publics. Many colleges and universities have scholarships, grants, and support services for veterans and their families. Some colleges have special courses to help veterans transition back to civilian life. *Military Times* magazine publishes an annual ranking of the top two- and four-year colleges for veterans. See the rankings at militarytimes.com.

Words of caution: education benefits are recruiters' best sales tools. The promise of low-cost college is appealing. But low-cost education shouldn't be the main reason for joining the military. There are wonderful benefits, but this is a very serious decision. It can be life changing (or life ending). Get any offer in writing, and then discuss it with your parents, your counselor, a coach, or other trustworthy adult *before* signing.

SUMMARY

Every branch of the military offers career opportunities and ways to fund college. Hundreds of thousands of young men and women are using military service as a way to serve their country and achieve their education goals – with little or no cash outlay. It isn't for everyone, but it may be perfect for you.

If you're serious about a college degree, get into ROTC or another program where you get your degree first. Then complete your military service after you graduate. People in these programs are more likely to earn degrees than those who complete military service before college. Many veterans who sign up for GI Bill tuition benefits don't use their full benefits. Some don't use their education benefits at all.

The military is also putting more emphasis on education than ever before. Degrees are necessary for many promotions. So, get your degree, and then serve.

CHAPTER 20 – LET YOUR EMPLOYER PAY

Many older (and some younger) students work full time and take advantage of employers' education programs to get degrees.

This is a great cost-saving strategy if you're energetic and patient. It takes many years to complete an undergraduate degree when you take one or two courses each semester. It also takes energy to work full time, plus attend classes, read, complete class assignments, take part in project teams, and study for exams.

If you're working full time, look into accelerated degree programs for working adults. (See Chapter 9 for more information.) You may also want to look at online competency-based degrees like Southern New Hampshire University's College for America. It is for working adults, with projects based on real-world work situations. (Read the next chapter for more information about competency-based degrees.)

According to Hewitt and Associates (a large human resources consulting firm), three of every four US employers offer education support programs. Education programs vary by employer. Different expenses qualify for reimbursement. Some employers pay 100 percent of the price of tuition, fees, books, and lab fees. Others offer partial payment of tuition. Some employers have no education programs at all.

Sometimes employers limit support to the college or university that provides the course at the lowest price. Some won't pay for online classes. Employers usually pay only for classes related to the organization. The amount often depends on how much the course applies to your current job.

Some employers cover only graduate-level courses. Others pay for all college courses. You must receive a passing grade. Sometimes you must earn at least a C or B. And occasionally, the amount you're paid depends on the grade you earn.

Most employers limit the number of classes or the amount they pay each year. The federal government allows you to receive up to $5250 in employer-provided education aid each year, tax free. You must pay income taxes on any amount above $5250.

You usually must take classes outside normal work hours. Some employers allow students to work on class projects related to their current jobs during work hours. A few companies, like United Technologies, allow employees to do some studying on company time. Others don't allow you to do any class assignments during work hours. Many have confidentiality or conflict of interest policies that keep you from using any company information for class projects.

Most employers provide education support only for full-time employees. Some offer scholarships to select employees. A few employers offer tuition reimbursement benefits for part-time employees. For example, UPS's Earn and Learn program is available at many locations in the US. It offers part-time management employees up to $5250 each year in tuition reimbursement, with a lifetime maximum of $25,000. And it's available to employees as soon as they start working at UPS!

Starbucks is another company that supports college education for part-timers who work twenty or more hours each week. The support is limited to Arizona State University (ASU) online bachelor's degree programs. ASU offers more than seventy undergraduate majors online. Starbucks pays full tuition for college juniors and seniors, and partial tuition for college freshmen and sophomores.

If your employer offers assistance to part-timers, it's possible you could work part time and carry a full college course load. If so, you might qualify for other financial aid, too.

Employers want to receive value from their investment in your education. So, if you leave shortly after you take a class, you may have to repay all or part of the benefits. Virtually all employers will consider you (after you graduate) for positions that require your new degree. If you're lucky, you'll get a raise, bonus, or other graduation gift.

Occasionally an employer will repay part of a new employee's student loans as a recruitment bonus. Employers usually offer this only to top job candidates in high-demand fields. You won't see anything on an employer's website about bonuses. You'd need to negotiate this after you have a job offer.

Some federal employees can have student loans repaid. The Federal Student Loan Repayment Program lets agencies repay federal student loans to recruit (or retain) employees. Federal agencies can make payments up to $10,000 per employee each year, with a maximum of $60,000. Each agency has its own rules and procedures for this program. If you're negotiating a job offer with the federal government, ask about it.

If you're interested in having an employer pay for your education, learn about the tuition assistance programs of your workplace or places you'd consider working. If employed, you can get details from the human resources department or from your company intranet (in-house website). If you want to find out about other employers, check their websites (search "education reimbursement") or talk with someone you know who works there. And when you interview for jobs, ask about education assistance. Also, be sure to get approval from your supervisor and human resources department *before* you register for a course.

SUMMARY

A great strategy to finance education is to work and take advantage of your employer's education program. Education support and good wages can help pay for college. If you have an opportunity to work for an organization with a strong education program, give it serious consideration.

I know hundreds of people who have taken advantage of employer education plans. Several of my employees accepted their jobs after they earned associate degrees. They used employer education support to complete bachelor's degrees while working full time. And I've had a few employees who started with the company right out of high school, and then completed bachelor's degrees while working full time.

I recently met a young woman who plans to use this strategy to finance her bachelor's degree and a graduate degree. She's currently in a dual enrollment healthcare academy. When she graduates high school, she'll have her CNA (certified nursing assistant) credential and several college credits toward a nursing degree. She plans to interview for jobs near her top-choice college, looking for organizations with good employee education benefits. She plans to get her RN (registered nurse) degree, paid in part by her employer. She hopes to use this same approach to get a graduate degree and become an advanced nurse practitioner.

Working and taking advantage of employer education benefits takes patience, energy, and hard work. But everyone I know who has used this approach to finance college enthusiastically supports it!

CHAPTER 21 – CONSIDER A COMPETENCY-BASED DEGREE

Have you heard of competency-based education? Have you wondered what it is?

At most colleges and universities, you earn a set number of credits to get your degree. The number of credits for a course depends on the time you're in class and the amount you're expected to study outside class. Students turn in assignments and take tests at the same time. Then anyone who passes the class earns the same number of credits. If you earn a passing grade, everyone assumes you've learned the important skills and knowledge.

However, everyone learns outside of classes. People learn on their jobs, through reading, and through hobbies. And you can learn free online from places like:

- YouTube (youtube.com)
- iTunesU (open.edu/itunes)
- Khan Academy (khanacademy.org)
- Open Education Consortium (oeconsortium.org)
- Carnegie Mellon's Open Learning Initiative (oli.cmu.edu)
- EdX (edx.org)
- Coursera (coursera.org)

Students who already know information or already have skills are frustrated if they must sit through classes on the same topics. They wonder, "Why do I have to *relearn* what I already know?"

Credit for prior learning, through exams like AP and CLEP, has been around for years. (See Chapter 8 for more information.) Most colleges will now let students earn some credits this way. Some schools base entire degrees on the student's ability to demonstrate skills and knowledge in a field. This is **competency-based education, CBE,** or **mastery-based learning**.

Schools use **direct assessment** of learning. By testing, reviewing your work, or watching you complete tasks, people decide if you have specific **competencies** (knowledge, skills, and abilities). Students earn competency-based degrees by proving they have skills, abilities, and knowledge – and can apply them.

In competency-based education, students move through courses at their own pace. Some people call this **self-paced instruction** or **personalized learning**. You progress as quickly (or as slowly) as you learn. If you're experienced, self-directed, learn quickly, and have time to study, you can likely earn a competency-based degree faster and less expensively than a traditional degree.

Most competency-based programs are online. Students can usually start classes at almost any time. This is especially helpful to people who lose jobs and want to start working toward a new career right away. Many programs charge **flat-rate tuition**. For example, a program might charge a fee every six months. It's a subscription service, like cable TV. With a **subscription**, you pay a fee for a period and use the service as much or as little as you want. In this case, you pay one amount and take as many classes as you want. So, the faster you advance, the less you pay for your degree. Some students can complete a bachelor's degree in two years. Of course, the opposite is also true – the slower you learn, the longer it takes, and the more you pay.

Many adults like self-paced classes. They speed through what they already know and spend more time learning new skills. Plus, they can devote less time to school when family and work responsibilities need attention.

However, some people question the value of competency-based education. If you plan to transfer competency-based credits, be sure they will transfer. And check about transferring credits *before* you enroll in the class. Transferring credits is rarely simple. But it's even more complex with competency-based credits.

Some graduate and professional schools don't recognize bachelor's degrees from competency-based programs. So, if you're planning to get a graduate degree, be sure the schools you're considering will accept your bachelor's degree.

There is a national push for more competency-based higher education. The pressure is coming from Congress, the Department of Education, and even the White House. So, there are a growing number of competency-based programs. And you can expect to see many more within the next few years.

Western Governor's University (WGU) is one of the oldest competency-based programs. WGU began offering competency degree programs in 1998. WGU is known for affordable, high-quality, online education. WGU offers competency-based degrees (at associate, bachelor's, and master's levels) in education, information technology, business, and healthcare. Numerous states support WGU, so students are often eligible for state, as well as federal, grant and loan programs. For more information about Western Governor's University, visit wgu.edu.

These schools all offer competency-based degrees (in some majors):

- Antioch University
- Argosy University
- Brandman University
- Broward College
- Capella University
- Charter Oak State College
- City University of Seattle
- DePaul University
- Excelsior College
- Kentucky Community/ Technical College System
- Lipscomb University
- Northern Arizona University
- Purdue University
- Salt Lake Community College
- Southern New Hampshire University
- Texas Higher Education Coordinating Board
- University of Maine at Presque Isle
- University of Maryland University College
- University of Michigan
- University of Wisconsin
- Westminster College

SUMMARY

If you're experienced, self-directed, learn quickly, and have time to study, you can likely earn a competency-based degree faster and less expensively than a traditional degree. Competency-based degrees are attractive to many working adults.

Work with a reputable, correctly accredited school. Make sure class credits transfer and apply toward your degree. If you are planning to study for a professional or graduate degree at another school, be sure the school will accept your bachelor's degree.

Chapter 22 – Consider
an Online Degree

If you're working full time, have young children, travel a lot, or live far from a college campus, consider earning an online degree.

Distance learning, where instructors and students are not together in classrooms, has been around for years. Your grandparents may have learned through correspondence classes. Your parents might have watched classes on videotapes. And now, with the Internet, colleges can offer classes whenever and wherever it's convenient for students. Even crews on submarines and arctic expeditions can earn distance degrees with today's technologies.

Nearly all schools offer some classes online. Many allow students to earn associate or baccalaureate degrees *completely* online. For example, Rochester Institute of Technology and Penn State's World Campus offer both associate and bachelor's online degrees. University of Maryland University College offers online bachelor's degrees with numerous majors and minors.

A few universities, like Jones International University and Capella University, are *totally* online. They don't have classroom buildings or traditional campuses.

Online classes can cut some costs for students. The biggest cost savings are on-campus living and commuting expenses. However, the prices for tuition, books, and supplies are usually similar to on-campus classes at the same school. They may even be higher. And online courses may charge technology fees or assessment fees that you wouldn't have if you were taking a class on campus. So, a student's main reason for choosing distance classes usually *isn't* to save money.

Flexibility and convenience are the major advantages in online learning. If you're working full time, it's usually easier to take classes online. In fact, some online classes require students to have jobs. Class assignments focus on real-world problems in the workplace.

Some online classes are synchronous, which means all students are involved at the same time. This allows real-time interaction among students and the instructor. Other classes are asynchronous, meaning you watch prerecorded sessions when convenient. Student and teacher interaction involves time delays in an asynchronous class.

Most synchronous classes meet during the evening. Asynchronous classes don't have a set meeting time. You're able to learn anytime. For example, you can work full time during the day and do classwork during your lunch break, in the evenings, or on weekends.

If you have young children, online education may be a good choice, especially if you live far from a college. Childcare costs can add a lot to total education costs. With online classes, you can study while children are asleep, at school, or with another adult.

Online learning is the only degree alternative with enough flexibility for some people. For example, people who travel a lot can attend class from almost anywhere. They just need a computer, web browser, and high-speed internet access. I recently read about a woman who is earning a degree while touring with an international ballet company. I also know an industrial service technician who is on call and must travel with little notice. He's completing an engineering degree online. And many soldiers and military spouses complete degrees online – all over the world!

If you work **rotating shifts** (sometimes called **swing shifts**, alternating between day and night hours) you're a good candidate for online education. You can attend class and study whenever your schedule allows. These jobs and those that require heavy travel often pay well. You get extra pay for your inconvenience. And many employers will pick up the cost for online classes, too. (Read Chapter 20 for more information.)

Online instructors are often part-time faculty with current work experience. Many students like the practical, up-to-date, real-world experience these teachers provide.

Online education may also be a good choice for people who can't study on a college campus. For example, I met a young man who was involved in his family's farming operation. His father was ill. So, he didn't feel he could leave the farm to go away to college. Online agriculture and business courses (which he completed at night) were a great solution. Plus, he could use what he was learning right away in the family business.

Online courses are also a good choice for people with physical limitations. For example, after a bad car accident my daughter completed college classes online. Online classes allowed her to study when she felt able. In addition, she didn't have to hobble around campus on crutches.

However, distance learning is not for everyone. You don't get face-to-face contact with your instructors and other students. And you don't get the out-of-class experiences that you get on campus. You don't go to concerts, football games, dances, or other traditional college activities. You focus on learning. That's not a bad thing, but it isn't for everyone. Online learning is best for mature, motivated, disciplined adults.

Online learning is not for people uncomfortable with technology. You need an up-to-date computer and reasonably high-speed internet connections. And you need enough technical ability to manage course software. You also need to type, email, create **pdfs** (a file format that produces an electronic image of words and/or graphics), and use video, text, and chat programs. However, most online schools have tutorials to help learn these skills, and technical support is available. Some have technical support **24:7** (twenty-four hours a day, seven days a week).

Many classes use a mix of online and in-person learning. Some call this **blended learning**. This allows students flexibility to do coursework when convenient. However, there are still occasional in-person sessions. A recent federal study found blended learning produced better results than *either* in-person or online classes alone.

In traditional college classes, people spend in-person time in lectures and do projects outside class. Some online learning programs reverse – or flip – that pattern. Students listen to lectures online and then work on projects in the classroom.

A word of caution: there are many low-quality online schools. So, know what you're buying. Check to see if a school is accredited and whether the accreditation is from a Department of Education-recognized organization. Some online schools aren't accredited. Others are accredited, but by agencies not recognized by the Department of Education. Most financial aid applies *only* at schools that have Department of Education-recognized accreditation. Check a school's accreditation at ope.ed.gov/accreditation.

Some ads promote online education as "the way to learn from the world's top professors." However, while top professors may lecture in online courses, they usually *aren't* the people who answer emails and interact with students.

If you plan to transfer online learning class credits, be sure they will transfer. And check about transferring credits *before* you enroll in the class. Transferring credits is rarely simple. But it's even more complex with online and other distance education credits.

Also, check to be sure distance classes count toward an on-campus degree from the same school. My daughter took distance classes from the same school where she'd been taking on-campus classes. Professors taught her classes. In addition, they used the same textbooks and assignments as on-campus classes. It never occurred to her (or me) that the online courses might not count toward graduation. However, that was the university's policy. Luckily, her department head finally stepped in and convinced the university to accept the distance course credits.

Some graduate and professional schools don't recognize bachelor's degrees from online or other distance education programs. So, if you're planning to get a graduate degree, be sure the schools you're considering will accept your bachelor's degree. If you don't know where you want to get an advanced degree, get your undergrad degree from a fully-accredited, on-campus program, to be safe.

If you have scholarships or grants, make sure they will cover distance classes. For some scholarships and grants, you must take all classes on campus.

To learn more about distance education visit individual college and university websites. Also, check:

- The US Distance Learning Association website (usdla.org)
- The Distance Education and Training Council website (detc.org)
- Peterson's Education Center (petersons.com)
- Distance-education.org.

SUMMARY

Distance education may provide flexibility needed to earn your degree. It is attractive to many working adults. Online classes are especially appealing to people who travel or have unpredictable work schedules. However, commuting and childcare costs are often the only cost savings.

If you want to try distance learning, work with a reputable, correctly accredited school. Make sure scholarships and grants will pay for the classes. Make sure class credits apply toward your degree and transfer, if needed.

In addition, if you are planning to study for a professional or graduate degree at another school, be sure the school will accept your bachelor's degree.

Chapter 23 – Figure Out Where to Apply

Have you decided where to apply? It's hard, but it's time to figure it out.

The past 22 chapters have outlined many different strategies you could use to afford college. I hope you've considered many options. As you were reading, some ideas probably sounded terrible. But many may have sounded good. Perhaps you took notes as you were reading and now have a list of good possibilities.

Write down some things you've decided about college. You probably have some "must haves" on your list – and some "nice to haves," too. These will be important as you begin the next part of your work. It's time to find schools that match your needs and then learn more about them. Then you'll pick four to eight colleges to which you'll apply.

You may already know a few places you want to apply. However, there are thousands of accredited colleges and universities – just in the US! If you want the best education at an affordable price, keep your options open until you consider many schools.

Our college and university system is huge and varied. Almost every student can find several great matches.

DECIDE THE IMPORTANT FACTORS

Start by listing the factors that are most important to you. A search engine can then help you find schools that match your needs. At this point, don't worry about cost.

- What types of schools interest you?
  Two-year, four-year, private, public?
- Is location important?
  Rural vs. urban, area of the country?
- Do you care how far a school is from your home?
- Is size important?
- What majors does the school need to offer?
- Are there certain sports or activities you want?
- Where do you want to live?
  On campus, off campus, at home?
- Do you want sororities, fraternities, or other clubs?
- Are there support services you need?
  Tutoring, veteran's center, or handicap accessibility?
- Do you care if there are many students like you?
  Race, ethnicity, sexual orientation, age, etc.?
- Do you want an honors program?
- Do you want a co-op program?
- Do you want to study abroad? (See Chapter 42)
- Do you want ROTC?
- Would you like internships? (See Chapter 41)
- Do you want an accelerated degree?
- Do you care whether the school is co-ed?
- Do you care if it has a religious connection?
- Do you need classes available nights or weekends?
- Do you want to take some (or all) classes online?
- Do you want a competency-based degree?
- Do you want credit for prior learning?
  AP, IB, CLEP, etc.?
- Is selectivity important to you?

USE COLLEGE SEARCH ENGINES

Once you have your list of important college characteristics (factors), use a free college search engine to help you find colleges that match them. It's like online dating. You enter facts about yourself (age, gender, high school GPA, ACT scores, SAT scores, etc.). You also enter important college characteristics. The search engine then returns schools that match your needs. One of the best free college search engines is at collegeboard.org. Others include:

- Collegeconfidential.com
- Collegedata.com
- College Navigator (nces.ed.gov/collegenavigator)
- Collegerealitycheck.com
- Collegeview.com
- Fastweb.com
- Petersons.com
- Whattheywilllearn.com

These use information from the Common Data Set. The **Common Data Set** is a collection of information from each college and university. Some search engines include other information, too. Search engines ask different questions, and identify match schools in different ways. So, try out several. (Read the terms and conditions to know what privacy you're giving up.) Also, look at Kiplinger's College Finder search engine (kiplinger.com). It focuses on 300 top-value schools. It includes graduation rates, net costs, and average debt of graduates. Finally, try out Linkedin's YOUNIVERSITY at linkedin.com/edu/university-finder. The Linkedin engine asks questions about what you want to study. It also asks about the type of employer you want and where you want to live.

Most search engines ask for your email address. If you give it to ACT, SAT, college searches, and scholarship searches, you will start getting a bunch of emails. You may want to set up new email accounts. I know one woman who set up three new (free) email accounts for college planning. One was for search engines. Another was for scholarship applications. The third was for correspondence with admissions and financial aid offices.

Search engines provide lists of colleges that match your needs. Once you have the lists, visit college websites to learn more. Narrow your list to 12-15 schools. Find out if schools have need-blind admissions and meet 100 percent of students' demonstrated financial need. Collect facts about average grade point averages and test scores of admitted students. This will be important as you decide where to apply, to get the best financial aid packages. If you don't find this information on a school's website, type "Common Data Set" into its search function. Then look at information from the most recent year.

GET ORGANIZED

As you narrow your list of colleges, get organized. Thinking about a dozen schools (or more) is confusing. Some people set up electronic files with a folder for each college and a spreadsheet for comparisons. If you're computer-savvy, electronic files are best, because most applications, correspondence, and submissions will be online. Always back up your files.

Other people keep things on paper. You might use big envelopes or folders with one for each school. On the outside, put the college name, key dates, and a list of everything you need to do.

CONSIDER VALUE

At this stage of the college search, some students feel overwhelmed. Some give up and just apply to a school that looks easy. However, that's not smart. You'll invest a lot of time and money getting your degree no matter where you go. You owe it to yourself to find great matches and to look closely at the value different schools provide.

So, what do we mean by "value?" **Value** compares the rewards of a decision with costs. Good value means benefits outweigh costs. Poor value means costs outweigh benefits. However, dollars can't always fully quantify rewards and costs. Enjoying college, graduating on time, and getting a job after you graduate are important rewards. The cost of attending schools includes time and other factors, as well as money.

However, you don't have a crystal ball! If you're looking for a formula that will tell you, with 100 percent certainty, that College X is *the* best choice for you, you won't find it – anywhere. Still, the more information you have, the better your decisions can be.

You cannot know exactly what you will pay for any college until the college offers admission and you get your financial aid award letter. The award letter tells you the financial aid the school will provide and your net price. Remember, net price is the difference between the sticker price (full cost) to attend the college for one academic year minus any grants, waivers, and scholarships.

Even though you won't know the exact prices until you get your award letters, you can get estimates of what each college will cost. Every college and university must provide a net price calculator on its website. Using the net price calculator, you can estimate your financial aid and your out-of-pocket expenses. It's helpful to have financial records (including your parents' records) with you when you use the calculators. You also need to know your high school GPA and ACT or SAT test scores. Use the same assumptions with each school's net price calculator so you can compare the prices. Read details the schools provide. They don't always provide the exact same information. Also, take notes or print out the information. Just remember, the net prices you calculate will be rough estimates, based on average students.

You can also use the net price calculator on College Board's website (netpricecalculator.collegeboard.org). With it, you can calculate the net prices of several schools. However, you might learn more using the calculators on individual school websites.

CONSIDER OUTCOMES

Next, look for information about **rewards** (sometimes called **outcomes measures, success factors**, or **performance results**).

- What percentage of students who start at the school stay?
- What percentage of students transfer?
- How many students graduate within four years?
- How many graduate within six years?
- What is the average debt students have at graduation?
- Are students able to repay their loans?
- How many students get jobs in their fields?
- How long does it take to find jobs?
- What is the average starting salary for those in your major?
- What do students say about the school?

Where can you find out answers to these questions? Colleges are becoming more **transparent** (open and honest) about outcomes. Look at information in the College Scorecards at the Department of Education's College Affordability and Transparency Center (collegecost.ed.gov). Also, look at collegeresults.org, a site from the Education Trust.

One factor to look for is **first-year retention rate** (the percentage of the school's freshmen who enroll the following year. For example, a student who studies full time during the fall semester and returns the next fall counts.) Some schools also provide **transfer-out rates**. These tell you the percentage of students who transfer to a different school.

Also, look at four-, five-, and six-year graduation rates. You might expect schools with similar admissions requirements (for example, GPA and test scores) to have similar graduation rates. However, they often don't. Schools might have similar incoming students. But one school might emphasize advising and class availability. Therefore, more students graduate within four years. For example, John Carroll University, a small school in Ohio, claims, "Our structure, culture, and environment make us successful at providing an outstanding education for our students. It helps them become John Carroll graduates in FOUR years. Not five. Not six. Four." A school with a high graduation rate might be a bargain compared with a similar school that costs less, but where it takes longer to earn your degree.

Collegeportraits.org also provides information to compare colleges. About 300 public colleges and universities take part. Each College Portrait includes characteristics of students and faculty, admission requirements, popular majors, average class size, campus safety, and plans of graduates. Every College Portrait includes a snapshot of student experiences based on questions from the National Survey of Student Engagement (NSSE or Nessie). Another website, ucan-network.org, provides similar information from more than 800 private, non-profit schools. Individual schools sometimes publish summaries from the National Survey of Student Engagement. Some schools also publicize their results from the College Senior Survey (CSS).

You can also gather information from published rankings. These include:

- *Money* magazine (time.com/money)
- *US News and World Report* (usnews.com/education)
- *Washington Monthly* (washingtonmonthly.com/college_guide)
- *Princeton Review* (princetonreview.com/college-education.aspx)
- *Kiplinger Report* (kiplinger.com)
- *Forbes* (forbes.com)

Before you look at the rankings, read about how they're determined. Different organizations rank colleges on different factors, just as individuals consider different factors when choosing a college. Factors may include the quality of education, outcomes, affordability, selectivity, research, and graduation rates. Look for rankings based on factors important to you. These websites provide free basic information. Review the complete reports at your local library. Just remember, none of these rankings is perfect. However, they all give you a little more information.

Data about graduates' employment and starting salaries is hard to find. For-profit schools must report information about jobs and student debt of graduates. One good example is CapellaResults.com, an online portal from Capella University. The site shares learning outcomes and career results. Future students can learn about other students' satisfaction and career progress.

Non-profit schools do not have to provide this kind of information. However, some colleges or departments choose to provide it on college or departmental websites. St. Olaf College, a private liberal arts school in Northfield, Minnesota, includes a section on its website (stolaf.edu/outcomes). It explains outcomes for recent graduates. Look for this kind of information on college websites. And ask about recent graduates' employment rates, average starting salaries, and other outcomes when you visit career services offices during college visits.

The Social Mobility Index (SMI), first released in the fall of 2014, ranks schools on outcomes for students whose families have incomes below the national median (midpoint). Rankings depend on published tuition, the percentage of students from lower income families, graduation rate, salaries 2.5 years after graduation, and the school's endowment. Learn more at socialmobilityindex.org.

Collegemeasures.org provides outcomes of two-year and four-year schools in several states. Information includes comparisons of student loan payments to earnings for recent graduates. The site links to a sister site in Texas, myfutureTX.com. The Texas site helps students learn about salaries for various occupations in that state. Students can find information about programs in Washington State at careerbridge.wa.gov. Other states are developing similar sites.

NerdWallet (nerdwallet.com) also has a tool that provides some student- and school-reported information on outcomes. It lets you see what graduates earn on average and the percentages employed or in graduate school. You can also find some information about the earnings of a college's graduates on payscale.com.

Based on information you gather, some schools will probably look better and some will look much worse. A low net price school might look less attractive if you find out it takes most students six years to graduate. On the other hand, a school with a high sticker price might look affordable after you see the net price you would likely pay.

VISIT YOUR TOP SCHOOLS

I hope you now have a list of colleges where you think you would do well and you'd be happy. If you have not visited your top colleges, figure out a way to go. College fairs are decent ways to collect information about many schools. But they don't replace in-person visits. College visits take time and they cost money. However, without a visit, choosing a college is like marrying someone you meet online, without ever meeting in person. You can't judge a college from its marketing materials. Visit, and talk with real students about their experiences.

Before you visit, sign up on the school's website, so people know you're coming. Take an official tour. But drop in on classes, too. Talk to students who are not official tour guides. Eat in a regular dorm cafeteria. Drop into the career services office. Ask questions.

College visits replaced family vacations when our children were in junior and senior high. Who doesn't dream of a vacation to Champaign, Illinois, or South Bend, Indiana? The teens were able to experience each campus and think about whether it might be a good fit.

If you're considering nearby schools, make sure you visit. If your family doesn't have a car, take public transportation. AMTRAK (the train company) offers college visit discounts. Or maybe you can carpool with a friend. Some high schools and colleges arrange group visits to campuses.

Private colleges have statewide Private College Weeks each summer. During those weeks, they host sessions for high school students and families. The tours include sessions about financial aid. Some schools pass out **application fee waivers**, so you can apply free. To learn about private college tours in your state, type "(state name) private college week" into your computer search engine or contact a private college admissions office.

Nearly all schools can arrange for an overnight stay. Some offer free meals, too. If your parent goes along, schools can provide a list of hotels with college visit rates. Occasionally, if a school really wants you, they'll pay your expenses to visit. We hear about athletes' campus visits. However, expense-paid visits are not just for athletes. Many schools pay expenses for high-potential, low-income student visits. If you can't afford to visit, ask admissions staff if money is available to help pay for a campus visit.

DECIDE WHERE TO APPLY

Once you have information collected, it's time to figure out where to apply. Narrow it down to four to eight schools. Compare costs versus rewards of schools you're considering. Only apply to schools where you think you would be happy and where you'd fit in academically. Ideally, they are schools you can afford (with scholarships, grants, and reasonable loans). However, if a school says it has need-blind admissions and commits to provide 100 percent of demonstrated financial need, don't worry whether you can afford it. If the school is a good fit, apply!

If you want maximum scholarship offers, apply to several schools. If you want merit-based aid, select schools where your grades and ACT/SAT scores are in the top 25 percent of students.

If you have top grades and test scores and you're a minority or first-generation student, aim high. Schools might offer you aid because you would help diversify their student body. According to David Coleman, the president of the College Board, many poor students with top SAT scores don't even apply to the most selective colleges. Don't be one of them! Aim high with some of your applications. Give yourself a chance!

If you won't qualify for need-based aid but you're an exceptional student, make sure your list includes some top public universities and second-tier (highly-selective, but not Ivy League) schools. If you *could* attend an Ivy League school, other schools will accept you and offer scholarships or grants.

Don't limit your applications to public schools thinking they'll offer the lowest price. The sticker prices of private colleges are higher than sticker prices of most publics. However, ignore the sticker price. The important price is the net price you'll pay.

So, apply to several schools you would like to attend. A good rule of thumb is to apply to one or two **safety schools** (where you are nearly certain to get in). Most public schools have lower GPA and test score requirements for in-state students. A safety school might also be an open-admissions school such as a community college. When you apply to out-of-state publics and privates, you're most likely to get in if your GPA and test scores are above those of average students. Remember, safety schools are more likely to offer you merit-based financial aid.

Apply to one or more schools where your test scores and GPA are like other students. These schools are good choices, especially if you'll qualify for need-based aid.

Also, apply to one or more **reach schools** where your GPA and test scores are below other students. Reach schools are *more* reachable if you're eligible for talent scholarships. If you're an exceptional athlete or musician, for example, you may be accepted and offered talent-based aid, even if your GPA and test scores are below those of other students.

And, if there's a school you've dreamed of attending, apply!

Be careful about applying *only* to safety schools. Everyone avoids rejection. So, it's easy to think, "I won't apply to College X. They wouldn't accept me, anyway."

Research shows minority and first-generation students are more likely to apply *only* to safety schools. Surprisingly, people who go to safety schools are *more* likely to drop out than those who attend reach schools. So, don't sell yourself short. If you're interested in a school, apply, even if it's a reach. Give yourself a chance!

SUMMARY

With good information, narrow your college choices. College search engines can help you consider your choices and narrow them down. Websites provide good information to help you decide which schools provide the best fit and value. Compare estimated net costs with the rewards you would expect if you attend. College visits can help you decide if a school is right for you.

Plan to apply to several schools. Most people should apply to at least four. The mix should include one or more safety schools and one or more reach schools. Once you have the list narrowed down, it's time for the important next step: apply! Apply to at least four schools, and apply for financial aid at every   school.

CHAPTER 24 – APPLY TO AT LEAST FOUR SCHOOLS

After considering many options, you've narrowed your choices. It's (finally) time to apply! You can cheat yourself out of financial aid if you only apply to one or two schools. Apply to several. Most people should apply to at least four schools. Some people apply to a dozen or more. But remember, each application takes time and money. You'll probably be much better off doing six great applications rather than a dozen lower-quality ones.

ADMISSIONS TERMS

Colleges and universities have **deadlines** (dates by which you need to do various things). Pay attention to **priority deadlines**. Colleges consider those who meet priority deadlines first. If the school has more slots available, they then consider those who apply after the priority deadline.

Regular decision is the name for the normal way to apply. It is usually the best way to apply to get financial aid. You file your application by a college's deadline and receive a decision by a given date or stated time. When you apply under regular decision, you can apply to other schools with no restrictions.

Some schools have **rolling admissions**. The school reviews applications as they come in. The school lets you know the admission decision right away. However, financial aid decisions are often separate, and most schools using rolling admissions do not send financial aid offers as soon as you're accepted.

With an **early decision** application process, you apply early (usually before November 1). You get an acceptance decision well ahead of the usual date. An early decision application indicates to the school that it is your top choice. Early decision is <u>not</u> a good approach if you are trying to save money on college. Early decisions are generally binding. If the school accepts you (and offers enough aid), the school expects you to enroll. In addition, you generally pay a nonrefundable deposit. You can apply to just one college early decision. You can still apply to other colleges under regular admission. If your first choice school admits you early decision, you must withdraw applications to other schools. So, read, understand, and be willing to stick with any restrictions if you apply early decision.

Early action is similar to early decision. However, it is not as restrictive. You usually learn early (January or February) if a college has accepted you. But most early action plans aren't binding. You can apply to other schools. However, if the school has **restrictive early action**, there may be limits on where you apply. Again, know and understand any restrictions before you apply early action.

Single-choice early action is another alternative. This works like other early plans. However, you may not apply early (either early action or early decision) to any other school. You can still apply to other schools regular decision. In addition, you do not have to accept any offer until the regular decision deadline. This lets you compare financial aid offers before deciding where to attend.

Some schools consider ability to pay as they consider whether to offer admission. Others do not. **Need-blind admission** means a college admits students without considering their ability to pay. Their admissions decision depends on your achievements and their expectation you will be successful. If a school considers your ability to pay as it decides whether to offer admission, it is **need-sensitive** (or **need-aware**). If a school does not say it has need-blind admissions, it will likely consider your ability to pay.

APPLY FOR ADMISSION <u>AND</u> FINANCIAL AID

Some schools consider every student for financial aid. Therefore, there is no separate financial aid application. However, many schools have two applications – one for admission and one for financial aid. In addition, you sometimes need to apply for individual scholarships. Read materials carefully. Make sure you apply for admission *and* for financial aid.

Complete all needed forms and meet every deadline. It's a lot to keep track of. So, develop a good system, and stay on top of it. Most applications and correspondence will be online, so you'll need electronic files. If you're keeping electronic files, set up a folder for each school. Back up your files.

If you're keeping paper copies, make a folder for each school. Write the school name, priority deadlines, and a list of things you have to submit on the outside. Gather necessary documents, and put copies in the folder. Check items off your list as you put them in. Then arrange folders by the earliest due date so you do not miss important deadlines.

Whether you're using electronic or paper files, make a master calendar of due dates. There will be many and you don't want to miss any deadlines.

Learn whether schools accept the **Common Application** (commonapp.org) or the **Universal College Application** (universalcollegeapp.com). If several schools accept these, you'll save time. It will also save time for people you ask for references and letters of recommendation. However, even if a school accepts a common application, it may require other school-specific forms and materials. For example, you may need to answer school-specific questions and write school-specific essays. You may also need to send official high school transcripts and official test scores to individual schools.

A useful feature on the Common Application website is the Application Requirements page. It summarizes college application deadlines, application fees, college testing requirements, and the number of required recommendations for each school.

Read instructions carefully and follow them. If you are to write an essay that includes fewer than 800 words, don't go over the limit. Most word processing programs have word count features.

Be truthful. Present yourself in the best light, but do not exaggerate or lie. Be honest about your grades, experiences, accomplishments, memberships, community service, leadership, qualifications, finances, and other information.

Keep answers to questions and copies of essays on your computer. Back it up. If you use a shared computer, save your answers on a USB flash drive. Keep the flash drive in a safe place. You can also save information on a shared internet server (such as the cloud). Many schools ask for similar information. Most ask about your high school accomplishments, leadership roles, college plans, career goals, etc. If you have answers handy on your computer, you can copy the file and not have to start over on every application. However, don't get sloppy. Be sure you answer every question thoroughly.

Many schools will require **references** or **letters of recommendation**. Adults (unrelated to you) answer questions or write statements about your character, work ethic, academics, and other factors that are important for college success. Choose reference providers carefully. Choose people who will say great things about you. Choose people who are reliable and who write well. Ask if they are willing to offer strong recommendations *before* listing their names. Don't overburden anyone. Allow plenty of time. Some teachers and counselors have rules about providing references. Follow them.

If you don't have specific instructions, provide information to recommenders at least three to four weeks before the deadline. A copy of your application or a resume is helpful. It will remind people of your accomplishments. They will also need the right forms, questionnaires, or questions to answer. The common applications let you invite recommenders to fill out forms online.

You may need to follow up to make sure schools get references and recommendations on time. About a week before the due date, politely ask the person if they have had time to complete the forms or write the letter. You don't want to be a pest, but you want to be sure these arrive on time.

If you're having trouble with your applications, send questions to the college admissions office. Your counselor may also know the answers. ACT and College Board websites are also good sources. EdX offers The Road to Selective College Admissions online – free. Sign up at EdX.org.

Proofread everything before you send it. Spell checking is not enough. Look for typos and grammatical errors. Have someone else read your applications and essays to offer suggestions. It's a good idea to type out your answers on a computer, using the spell-check and grammar-check features. Then print them out and proofread again. Once you're satisfied, cut and paste answers into the online application. Proofread one more time before you hit the "send" button.

Try to send everything ahead of deadlines. Make sure nothing is late. Everything must follow the rules exactly. For example, if the application requires an official high school transcript with your school's seal, do not send a photocopy. Follow instructions exactly.

If you submit an application electronically, you'll get a confirmation email. It tells you the school received your application. Put a copy of the confirmation in your folder for that school.

SAVE MONEY ON APPLICATIONS

You have to spend a bundle to apply to colleges, right? Wrong. Every student who plans can limit application expenses. Low-income students can eliminate almost all application expenses. College application fees average around $50. Some colleges charge up to $100. The fee is usually nonrefundable, even if you aren't accepted. However, if you're from a low-income family, most schools will waive application fees. If you apply to several schools, each charging $50 or more, application fee waivers can mean big savings.

High school counselors, college recruiters, and representatives at college fairs usually know if a college offers fee waivers. The Common Data Set questionnaire also tells whether a school waives application fees for low-income applicants. Type "Common Data Set" into the search feature of the school's website. Look at the Admission Policies section of the most recent report. If it says the school waives application fees for low-income applicants, find out how to get the waiver. You can usually find details in the application section of the school's website. Otherwise, contact the admissions office.

You can usually have application fees waived if:

- You're eligible to receive an ACT or SAT fee waiver.
- You're eligible for free or reduced-price lunches.
- Your family qualifies for the Supplemental Nutrition Assistance Program (SNAP), often called food stamps.
- You're in a federal, state, or local program that helps students from low-income families (for example, TRIO programs like Upward Bound).
- Your family gets public assistance.
- You live in federally-subsidized public housing, a foster home, or are homeless.
- You're a ward of the state or an orphan.

To get a fee waiver, your counselor or college advisor must submit an admissions fee waiver application. The Common Application, the National Association of College Admissions Counselors (NACAC), the College Board, and ACT supply these forms to counselors. Some schools also accept letters from representatives of social service or community agencies stating the fee would cause financial hardship for you. (These are important for adult students.) It takes effort to get application fee waivers. But each fee waiver can save you $50, or more! If you're applying to four colleges, it's an easy way to save $200.

Many colleges even have fee waivers for students who are not low-income. For example, some schools waive fees for military veterans. College recruiters who visit high schools and college fairs often have fee waivers for students. If you're talking to a recruiter and the school looks interesting, don't be shy. Ask if you can get an application fee waiver.

If you participate in Private College Week visits, you may get application fee waivers to some schools. Some states have a College Application Week (or month) in October or November. Some colleges in the state waive application fees if you apply at that time. Look for posters and other announcements about College Application Week.

You'll save money if you apply online. You can apply online to almost all US schools. If you send bulky applications to several colleges (especially if you've waited until the last minute), postage and shipping fees add up.

A word of caution: don't get sloppy with your application or correspondence. Every email or text message you send is important. Send well-composed, spell-checked, and proofed messages. Save money online, but don't get sloppy.

Also, if the deadline for applications is 11:59 p.m. on December 15, don't wait until the evening news to finish your application. You'll get sloppy. In addition, servers often slow down with heavy traffic before deadlines. Avoid the last minute rush with online applications.

PREPARE FOR AUDITIONS AND INTERVIEWS

If invited to an audition or interview, prepare. Think about how you'll respond to questions.

- Why do you think this school is right for you?
- How have you gathered information about colleges?
- Why would you be an asset to our freshman class?
- What are your career goals?
- What is your greatest strength?
- What are your weaknesses?
- What will be your biggest challenge in college?
- Who is the most influential person in your life?

Ask a parent, teacher, or counselor to **role-play** (practice) with you. It'll help you think about answers and become more comfortable. Don't try to memorize answers. It can make you sound like a robot. Try to develop clear and thoughtful responses. Also, think of questions you'd like to ask. Go into the interview well groomed, well rested, confident, and willing to show the interviewer(s) what a good person you are. Thank interviewers for their time and consideration.

SUMMARY

Invest the time, energy, and application fees to apply to several schools. Apply regular decision and for financial aid at every school. Remember, applications for financial aid are often separate from admissions applications. Apply for both.

Complete required forms and proofread everything before sending. Read carefully for typos and grammatical errors. Try to send everything ahead of the deadlines. Make sure nothing is late.

If you plan, you can save money on college applications. You can avoid postage fees. Plus, you can often eliminate application fees, especially if you're from a low-income family.

CHAPTER 25 – APPLY FOR GRANTS AND SCHOLARSHIPS

Are grants and scholarships worth the effort? Absolutely! Get as much scholarship and grant aid as possible. You don't have to pay scholarships and grants back (as long as you meet the conditions). Therefore, it's free money! It's even better than winning the lottery. If you win the lottery, you get money. However, you have to pay taxes on it. You don't have to pay taxes on most scholarships and grants!

START SEARCHING EARLY

Start searching for grants and scholarships about the time you start looking at colleges. Your sophomore year of high school is not too soon to start learning what's available. Start working on applications a year before college. Most grants and scholarships are for academic years, starting each fall. If you start school in the spring or summer, there may not be as many scholarships available right away.

Scholarships have early deadlines. Some are even before college application deadlines! For example, Wendy's High School Heisman applications are due in early October senior year of high school. Horatio Alger Scholarship applications are also due in October. Applications for the Coca-Cola Scholars Program are due October 31.

CONSIDER TAKING THE PSAT

If you're a strong student, your first scholarship event is the Preliminary SAT/National Merit Scholarship Qualifying Test (PSAT/NMSQT). It's the first step of the National Merit Scholarship. It's also the first step for the National Achievement Scholarship (for Black American high school students). Students take the PSAT/NMSQT during their junior year. You sign up through your counselor or principal at the beginning of the school year and take the test in October. So, if you plan to start college in the fall of 2017, you take the test in October 2015. The fee for the PSAT/NMSQT is about $15. Some schools charge extra to cover administrative expenses. Eleventh graders from low-income families can get a fee waiver. If you qualify for free or reduced-price school lunches, you can get a fee waiver. See your counselor. If you're home-schooled or your school doesn't offer the test, you can take it at another school. Some sophomores also take the test for practice. Fee waivers are not available for sophomores.

The odds of getting a National Merit Scholarship are low. Only about one in 100 students who take the test earn the scholarship. In addition, even if you get one, you may not get much money from National Merit. However, doing well on the test opens other doors. For example, some schools, such as the University of Oklahoma, offer full scholarships to National Merit finalists. (About two in 100 students who take the test become finalists.) At Oklahoma, these students don't just get a scholarship. They also get special advising, admission to the Honors College, study abroad opportunities, and the chance to do undergraduate research. Oklahoma also waives their tuition for five years. Therefore, some people use the scholarship to get their bachelor's degree, and then start graduate school.

Some corporations also sponsor scholarships based on National Merit results. Corporations often give scholarships to employees' children or students in communities where they're located. PSAT/NMSQT shares results with other scholarship programs. For example, the National Hispanic Recognition Program (NHRP), National Scholarship Service, and the Telluride Association get PSAT/NMSQT results.

When you take the PSAT/NMSQT, you also practice for the SAT. The tests are very similar. The College Board, which offers both the PSAT and SAT, has a feature on their website called My College QuickStart. You can use PSAT results to get personalized college planning help on that site.

However, taking the PSAT/NMSQT is just the beginning of your scholarship search. National Merit is just one of thousands of scholarship programs.

DIFFERENT TYPES OF SCHOLARSHIPS AND GRANTS

There are different kinds of grants and scholarships. Many people use these terms are interchangeably. They are very similar. However, grants usually depend more on financial need. Scholarships often depend on other factors, including merit and/or talent.

Grants tend to be less competitive than scholarships. If students meet the minimum conditions, apply, and there is money available, they usually receive grants. The **grantor** (government, school, or other organization giving the money) awards grants to many qualified **grantees** (students). With scholarships, a student must meet the conditions and apply. The scholarship provider compares all applications. The provider then awards the scholarship to only one or a few of the top applicants.

Need-based scholarships depend on a family's lack of money for college. For scholarships based on financial need, you need to complete the Free Application for Federal Student Aid (FAFSA). Need-based scholarships and grants sometimes also require the CSS Financial Aid PROFILE. Read the next chapter for details about the FAFSA and PROFILE.

Other scholarships and grants are merit-based. Merit-based scholarships depend on your academic record. Your **academic record** includes several parts. One part is your high school grade point average (GPA). Another is your set of high school classes. Scholarship agencies look for students who have taken challenging college prep classes and done well. If you have taken honors and Advanced Placement classes, it's a plus. College admissions (ACT and SAT) test scores are also considered. If you take both tests, send your highest score. These tests use different scales, so the numbers don't match up. You can see how the scores compare by looking at the ACT website (act.org). Search "ACT and SAT concordance." Teacher recommendations and academic awards (such as science fairs, math contests, and spelling bees) also count for merit-based scholarships. Most merit-based scholarships also consider community service. They reward students who are involved in clubs, school activities, and youth groups.

Some grants and scholarships consider only financial need. Some only consider merit. However, many consider *both* merit and financial need. Some consider other factors, such as your family background. Black Americans, Latinos, and those in other minority groups have special scholarship opportunities. Some scholarships target students who are the first in their families to attend college. Others, such as the Horatio Alger Scholarship (horatioalger.com), target people who have overcome difficulties. Some scholarships are just for adults who start or return to college later in life. Whoever provides money for the scholarship sets the rules for selection. They decide on the factors and the **weight** (importance) of each factor.

Another kind of scholarship is talent-based. Athletic scholarships are the best known. Students in debate, speech, and other non-athletic teams can also get scholarships. Almost any team that competes with other colleges has scholarships. Students who participate in the arts can also get talent-based scholarships. For example, schools offer art, drama, dance, symphony, creative writing, and marching band scholarships to talented students. Most of these are not large scholarships, but there are a lot of them.

Were you the president of your student council or the editor of the yearbook in high school? If so, and you're interested in continuing in college, you may be in luck. Some schools offer a tuition discount or scholarship to student government leaders or to the editors of the college newspaper and yearbook.

FIND SCHOLARSHIPS AND GRANTS

You've possibly heard stories about the millions of dollars in scholarships that go unclaimed every year. Do not believe them! There are no big scholarship checks just lying around waiting for you to pick them up. Work hard to find and apply for scholarships. It takes time and effort to fill out applications and meet deadlines. Just a few of the people who apply actually get one.

People rarely "win" scholarships. They earn them! You earn scholarships by working hard in high school, by searching out scholarship opportunities, and by making your applications as good as possible. However, it can be worth the effort. Remember, scholarships and grants are free money. Even small scholarships add up. I know a young woman who pieced together fifteen different scholarships to help pay for her first year of college. They were all small scholarships, but together they kept her from having to borrow.

For most scholarships, you complete an online application. You must also provide official high school transcripts and official ACT or SAT test scores. You often have to write essays and get recommendations from teachers. For scholarships based on your athletic ability or talent, you submit a collection of your work or a video of performances. The final stages of many scholarship competitions include in-person interviews or auditions. Therefore, scholarship applications can take as much, or even more, effort than college applications. If you have not started looking for scholarship opportunities by the summer after your junior year in high school, make it your summer project. It's a lot of work, but it can be worth it.

Your first project is to find scholarships matches – scholarships for which you are eligible. There are many free ways to find this information. Therefore, you should never pay someone to find scholarship opportunities.

USE SCHOLARSHIP SEARCH ENGINES

The best place to start looking is a free online search engine. Most of them work about the same way. However, their sources of information are different, so they give different results. Try using these scholarship searches:

- Collegeboard.org
- Fastweb.com
- Scholarships.com
- Petersons.com
- Dollarsforscholars.org

These have up-to-date information. They also offer reasonable protections for personal information. Read about what they do with your information, so you can make informed decisions about using these sites. Most of these sites also provide scholarship advice. For example, some have articles about writing essays. At scholarshipamerica.org, you can download a free copy of *The Scholarship Coach* ebook. It includes information about scholarships and tips for applications.

Complete questionnaires (including optional questions) on the scholarship search engines. The search engines should give you good information about national scholarships. However, they will not have much about local scholarships. And, those are the ones you have the best chance of getting. The fewer people who apply for a scholarship, the more likely you'll get it. So, don't focus all your efforts on big-name, high-dollar scholarships that everyone else is chasing. Invest time and energy finding and applying for smaller, lesser-known scholarships, too.

FIND SCHOLARSHIPS AT YOUR TOP SCHOOLS

Start out learning about scholarships and grants offered at schools where you're applying. Look in financial aid sections of college websites. Explore the types of scholarships and grants available. All kinds of colleges, including community colleges and online schools, offer grants and scholarships.

Almost all schools offer need-based scholarships and grants. Non-federal, need-based scholarships often consider academic merit (such as high school GPA, class rank, and test scores), too. Most colleges and universities also have merit- and talent-based scholarships. You'll have the best chance of getting merit-based awards if your GPA and test scores are higher than the typical student at that school.

FIND SCHOLARSHIPS FOR YOUR MAJOR OR CAREER

Next, explore scholarships tied to the major you're considering. These scholarships might be on department websites rather than on the school's main website. For example, there may be scholarships for biomedical engineering students that don't appear on the university's main web pages.

Next, think about scholarships tied to the career you're planning. Many professions, such as nursing, advertising, engineering, or teaching, offer scholarships. Local, regional, and national professional groups sponsor these. Start with an internet search to find out the names and websites of professional groups. Some professions have one national association, but others have more. Find the websites of professional groups in your career field, and then search "college," "student," and "scholarships." The national websites may provide contact information or web links for a local chapter in your area. These local chapters may offer scholarships beyond those on national websites.

The US is facing a shortage of people with STEM (science, technology, engineering, and math) training. Therefore, there are many scholarships for talented students interested in these fields. Sometimes students complete science or technology projects and enter competitions. The Siemens Competition has some of the biggest scholarships. Students register as individuals or in teams. The scholarships for top projects range from $1000 to $100,000. If you are interested in scientific research, this might be a great opportunity for you. Visit discoveryeducation.com/siemenscompetition for more information. Intel's Science Talent Search is a similar competition. The competition awards forty students $7500 to $100,000 based on their research projects, interviews with judges, academic records, and recommendations. Find out more at student.societyforscience.org. There are other STEM scholarships besides Siemens and Intel. When you enter personal data (such as gender, race, GPA, test scores, college major, and career plans) into college search engines, you'll find ones for which you're eligible.

Another scholarship program that targets students interested in STEM careers is the National Co-op Scholarship Program. Each year it awards nearly 200 merit-based scholarships, worth nearly $5 million, to students who want to participate in co-operative education at one of eleven member schools. Learn more about cooperative education and this scholarship program in Chapter 14.

FIND SERVICE-BASED SCHOLARSHIPS

If you know you want to teach or work in healthcare or education and are willing to work in a specific location, you may qualify for programs that help pay for school or pay back student loans. However, even if called scholarships, these programs work more like loans. To forgive (cancel) a loan, you have to hold up your end of the bargain. If, for some reason, you cannot (or change your mind and do not want to) meet your obligations, you have to repay the loan *and* interest. To learn more about service scholarships, read Chapter 29.

FIND TALENT-BASED SCHOLARSHIPS

Are you outstanding at any sports? According to the National Collegiate Athletic Association (NCAA), only about two percent of high school athletes earn college scholarships. However, if you are exceptional, you might be one of them. We often think of NCAA Division I football and basketball scholarships and the players we see on TV. However, athletic scholarships are also available at smaller schools and for lesser-known sports. For example, there are scholarships for rowing, gymnastics, water polo, track, volleyball, hockey, wrestling, and fencing. The NCAA (ncaa.org) and the National Association of Intercollegiate Athletics (NAIA) (naia.org) provide information for students and parents. Go to these websites to learn about eligibility, scholarships, and the process to get athletic scholarships. If you want to be a student athlete at a Division I or II school, you need to register with the NCAA Eligibility Center. The NCAA Eligibility Center certifies the academic and amateur status of college-bound student athletes. The NAIA Eligibility Center provides a similar service for students who want to attend schools with smaller intercollegiate athletic programs. Both eligibility centers offer fee waivers for low-income students.

Do you have other strong talents? Activities that have competitions with other colleges or arts activities have scholarships. Musicians who sit "first chair" in university symphonies, key members of bands, good actors, dancers, debaters, majorettes, and drum majors sometimes get scholarships. Some schools have talent-based scholarships for voice, art, and creative writing.

FIND LOCAL ORGANIZATIONS THAT FUND SCHOLARSHIPS

Do you belong to clubs or groups that award scholarships? Many clubs and religious groups have scholarships through local, regional, and national organizations. Schools started by a religious group often have grants or scholarships for members of their faith. They also provide scholarships to those who want to become ministers.

Some local and regional community service groups provide scholarships to non-members. Local chapters of the American Legion, Elks, Optimists, Rotary International, Pilot, Lions, Kiwanis, Tri T, and Junior League offer scholarships.

Dollars for Scholars is a national network of over 1100 community-based scholarship foundations. These are in cities and towns throughout the United States. Dollars for Scholars depends on community members giving money to help area students attend college. Dollars for Scholars offers many small scholarships. Therefore, if there is a chapter in your town, you have a good chance to get a small first-year scholarship. Check out the national website (scholarshipamerica.org) to see if there is a chapter in your area. The Dollars for Scholars website also provides free information about scholarships and the college planning process.

Think about where your parents work. Many large companies offer scholarships for employees' children. Ask your parents to check with human resources departments to see what might be available.

Sometimes major employers offer scholarships to local students even if their parents do not work for the company. For example, electric and gas power companies often offer scholarships to students in their service areas. Many fast food chains, department stores, and supermarkets that employ teenagers offer scholarships, too.

If your parent or guardian is dead, check with former employers. Even though my father died before I started high school, I was eligible for (and received) a college scholarship from Meredith Corporation, where he had worked. If your parent was killed working as a firefighter, police officer, or soldier, there are many scholarships available to you.

Do your parents belong to any unions, sororities, professional groups, fraternities, or clubs? Unions and membership groups sponsor many scholarships. For example, the unionplus.org website lists scholarships available to union workers and their children. Ask your parents to check with the organization's leaders to see if scholarships are available.

Some high schools even have their own scholarships. Parent groups or wealthy graduates give money for these.

Brainstorm with your parents, friends, coaches, teachers, and counselor about scholarships for which you might be eligible. Then start gathering information. Most high schools have an awards ceremony each spring to recognize scholarship recipients and other seniors. Get a copy of the program (or newspaper article) about your school's assemblies for the past few years. They may list students who earned scholarships and names of scholarship organizations.

CONSIDER STATE AND CITY SCHOLARSHIPS

Almost every state has grants and scholarships for residents. However, these awards normally apply only to students who attend college in state. The National Association of Student Financial Aid Administrators (NASFAA) has links on its website (nasfaa.org) to financial aid groups in each state.

A few programs offer large scholarships to students who graduate high school in a specific city. These include the Kalamazoo (Michigan) Promise, the Pittsburgh (Pennsylvania) Promise, and Say Yes to Education in Syracuse, New York. If you are lucky enough to live in one of these cities, take advantage of the opportunity!

APPLY FOR MINORITY AND FIRST-GENERATION
SCHOLARSHIPS, IF YOU QUALIFY

There are some scholarships for first-generation college students and students of ethnic groups under-represented on college campuses. The Gates Millennium Scholarships, for example, go to about 1000 low-income minority students each year. Academic achievement, community service, and leadership potential are keys to these awards. Outstanding African American, American Indian/Alaska Natives,

Asian/Pacific Islander Americans, and Hispanic American students earn these awards. People interested in studying computer science, education, engineering, library science, mathematics, public health, or the sciences get special consideration. You can submit personal information, but an adult (such as a counselor or school administrator) must nominate you for this award. Relatives cannot nominate you or serve as a reference. Gates Millennium Scholars get financial support each year of their undergrad and graduate degrees, as long as they make good progress. The scholars also take part in leadership programs and get personal and academic support throughout college. Find out more at gmsp.org.

If you are African American, check out opportunities on the United Negro College Fund website (uncf.org). The United Negro College Fund provides scholarship (and internship) opportunities for African American students. It also provides financial support for many Historically Black Colleges and Universities (HBCUs). At one time, most African Americans could *only* go to college at these schools. African Americans have many choices today, including HBCUs. Fisk University in Nashville, Morehouse College and Spellman College (both in Atlanta), and Tuskegee University in Tuskegee, Alabama, are excellent HBCU schools. The United Negro College Fund provides scholarships to those who attend HBCUs and more than 850 other schools. See uncf.org for a list of more than 400 scholarships, plus eligibility and application information.

The Hispanic Scholarship Fund (HSF) provides many scholarships. To be eligible, you must be a US citizen (or legal permanent US resident) of Hispanic heritage. You must have a 3.0 or higher GPA and enroll full time in a degree program at an accredited US college or university. You can start at a community college, but you must plan to complete a bachelor's degree. You must also complete the FAFSA and qualify for federal aid. To learn more visit hsf.net. The Hispanic Association of Colleges and Universities (HACU) also provides scholarships to Hispanic students who attend one of nearly 250 member schools. Visit the student section of hacu.net for more information.

If you are a Native American, you may want to attend a Tribal College. Tribal Colleges are often on remote reservations. They serve American Indian communities with limited access to other schools. At a Tribal College, you would study native culture along with traditional academic subjects. Most Tribal Colleges offer associate degrees. The American Indian College Fund provides scholarships to Tribal Colleges based on your academic record, financial need, and community involvement. Other scholarships are available to Native Americans through the American Indian College Fund. Students can use these scholarships at any accredited public or non-profit college in the US. To learn more, visit collegefund.org. Many other colleges and universities have departments or centers for Native American or American Indian studies and offer need-based and/or merit-based scholarships.

The Asian and Pacific Islander American Scholarship Fund (apiasf.org) provides scholarships for Asian Americans and Pacific Islanders. The organization's website also links to other scholarships targeted to Asian Americans and Pacific Islander Americans.

FIND SCHOLARSHIPS FOR ADULTS

Adults have many scholarship and grant opportunities. Most scholarships do *not* have age limits. In addition, there are scholarships that target adult students. For example, the Talbots Women's Scholarship Program (managed by scholarshipamerica.org) offers more than thirty scholarships for adult women. The Jeanette Rankin Foundation (rankinfoundation.org) also targets scholarships to adult women. So, look for scholarship opportunities, whatever your age. If you have lost a job, there are also federal and state grants that help people train for new jobs and careers. Check with your local unemployment or workforce development office. Also, check with your local community college.

Some groups also offer scholarships to spouses of employees. For example, spouses (and children) of federal employees with three or more years of service are eligible for scholarships through the Federal Employee Education Assistance Fund (feea.org).

Are you a military veteran? Many schools offer tuition discounts to veterans. Some offer discounts to spouses and children of veterans, too. In addition, many offer special scholarships. These groups do, too:

- Blinded Veteran's Association (bva.org)
- Military Order of the Purple Heart (purpleheart.org)
- National Military Family Association (nmfa.org)
- Armed Forces Communications and Electronics Association (afcea.org)
- Paralyzed Veterans of America (pva.org)

GET ORGANIZED

Get organized as you work on scholarships. Your system should be similar to your college application system. Make files for national, state, and local scholarships for which you are eligible. Include the name and address, selection factors, application details, and due dates. Make a note if they are just for college freshmen or if students can apply at other times. (You'll need this information later.) Include deadlines for references, tests scores, etc.

Make sure you meet all scholarship guidelines before you spend time and energy filling out applications. I have participated on dozens of scholarship committees. I am always amazed at how many people apply who do not meet basic eligibility requirements. Sometimes they live in the wrong community. Or they don't plan to major in the right field. If you do not match the eligibility factors, save your time and energy. Focus on scholarships for which you are eligible.

Set aside time to produce impressive, error-free applications. Try to understand what the scholarship is rewarding before you start answering questions. For example, the Wendy's High School Heisman focuses on athletics, academics, and service. Therefore, you would highlight these areas in your application.

The person who has done the most "stuff" does not earn scholarships. Highlight your activities that relate to the scholarship. If the scholarship is from a group that promotes specific values, be cautious. You want your application to show that your values are consistent with the scholarship and the sponsoring organization. If a scholarship focuses on talents, or career interests, stress your goals. Emphasize how you are working to achieve your full potential.

Read instructions carefully, and follow them. If you are to write an essay of no more than 600 words, do not exceed 600 words!

Do not get sloppy. Be sure you are answering each application's questions thoroughly.

Be truthful. Present yourself in the best light, but do not exaggerate or lie. Be honest about your grades, experiences, accomplishments, memberships, community service, leadership, qualifications, and finances.

Choose references carefully. Start this early, because the coaches, teachers, mentors, and employers you will be asking for recommendations are busy. You want to make sure they have time to write quality, thoughtful recommendations. Choose people who are reliable and who write well. Choose people who will say great things about you. Ask references if they are willing to offer strong letters of recommendation *before* you list their names. Do not overburden one person with many requests. Allow them plenty of time.

Give references copies of your application or resume. It will remind them of your accomplishments. Some general information about the scholarship is also good, so they can tailor comments, just as you are doing. They also need the right forms, questionnaires, or questions they need to answer. If they need to mail references, provide addressed envelopes with the right postage attached.

You may need to follow up to make sure they send their comments on time. You do not want to be a pest, but you also want to be sure that references arrive before deadlines.

Keep answers to scholarship questions and copies of essays on your computer. If you're using a shared computer, save answers to a USB flash drive or save them on the Internet.

Many scholarships ask for similar information. Most ask about your high school accomplishments, leadership roles, college plans, and career goals. Therefore, if you have answers handy, you can copy the text and not start over with every application.

Proofread everything before you send it. Spell check is not enough. Read thoroughly for typos and grammatical errors. Ideally, have someone else read it and offer suggestions, too.

Try to send everything ahead of deadlines. Make sure nothing is late. Scholarship groups usually will not consider your application if anything is late, even if it is not your fault. Some financial aid applications have priority deadlines. Priority deadlines for scholarships and other financial aid are like those for admissions. Colleges and scholarship agencies consider those who meet priority deadlines first. *If* they have any financial aid leftover, they *may* consider those who apply after the priority deadline.

When you submit an application online, you will get a confirmation message. Put a copy in your scholarship folder. If you mail the application, take it to the post office. Ask about the best way to send it to get it there on time. Pay a little extra to get a delivery confirmation so you know that it got there.

PREPARE FOR AUDITIONS AND INTERVIEWS

If invited to an audition or interview, think about how you'll respond to potential questions. Review the questions suggested in the last chapter. Also:

- Why should we award this scholarship to you?
- How would it change your college experience?
- Who is your role model?
- What is your favorite book? Why?
- Tell me about a time you displayed leadership.
- What world event this year has most affected you?
- If you had a million dollars, what would you do with it?

Ask a parent, teacher, or counselor to role-play (practice) with you. It will help you think about answers and become more comfortable. Try to develop clear and thoughtful responses. Before the interview, think of questions that you would like to ask. Go into the interview well groomed, well rested, and confident. At the end of the interview, thank the interviewers for their time and consideration.

SAY THANK YOU!

Be sure to thank everyone who helps you with scholarship applications. Be sure to thank the sponsors, too. Someone has given up his or her hard-earned money to provide you with an opportunity. They've placed their confidence in you. Tell them how much you appreciate it!

CONDUCT AN ONGOING SCHOLARSHIP SEARCH

Many people think of the scholarship hunt as a one-time event. It isn't! It needs to be ongoing throughout college. So, keep your scholarship files. It will save time the following year. Stay alert for new opportunities. Watch for them on bulletin boards and in financial aid newsletters and websites. Reread this chapter each summer and start an annual scholarship hunt.

Some scholarships are multiyear awards (sometimes called **renewable scholarships)**. However, even these are not automatic. You will get money each year *only* if you meet the scholarship guidelines. You have to keep a minimum GPA and be making satisfactory progress toward your degree. If a scholarship depends on a specific major, you have to stick with it. In addition, if it depends on financial need, you must file a FAFSA (and possibly a PROFILE) every year. Check what you must do to renew your scholarships after the first year. In addition, make sure you meet all deadlines.

SUMMARY

Start searching for scholarship and grant opportunities about the same time that you begin looking at colleges (at least one year before you plan to start college). Make it your goal to get as much scholarship and grant aid as possible. Apply for any scholarships for which you are eligible, even small ones.

Always get scholarship forms completed accurately and sent early. Colleges, universities, and scholarship groups will not accept late applications. In addition, they only have a set amount of aid to award. Schools often make financial aid awards on a first come, first served basis. When the money is gone, it is gone.

If you want the maximum amount of scholarships and grants, keep searching and applying as you progress through college. Reread this chapter each summer and start your annual scholarship hunt. And make sure you do everything needed to keep your multiyear, renewable scholarships and grants.

CHAPTER 26 – COMPLETE THE FAFSA AND PROFILE

For grants and scholarships based on financial need, you must complete the Free Application for Federal Student Aid (FAFSA). You sometimes also need the CSS/Financial Aid PROFILE. It is very important to complete these early and correctly. Some schools and scholarships have deadlines in early February. Set aside time in January to complete federal income taxes and then the FAFSA and PROFILE.

FILE AS SOON AFTER JANUARY 1 AS POSSIBLE

Federal financial aid such as grants, loans, and Work-Study use the FAFSA. Even if you don't think you will qualify for federal aid, complete it. Some people know they will not get a Pell grant, so they think the FAFSA can't help them. Wrong! State governments, individual colleges, and private groups also use FAFSA data to award need-based grants and scholarships. Some state grants are much larger awards than Pell grants. And, some are available to students with higher family incomes. In addition, some schools will not consider you for *any* scholarships if you have not completed the FAFSA. In addition, the government uses FAFSA data to decide if you're eligible for federal college loans. So, complete the FAFSA.

File your FAFSA every year you plan to attend college. It is not a one-time application. Federal financial aid award years are not calendar years (January 1 through December 31). If you want federal aid for the 2015-2016 award year (July 1, 2015 - June 30, 2016), complete a 2015-2016 FAFSA. If you plan to take classes during summer, check with the financial aid office to see which FAFSA form you should complete. The form and information about the FAFSA is online at fafsa.ed.gov. File after your family completes its federal income taxes or by your earliest college (or scholarship) financial aid deadline. College deadlines are earlier than income tax deadlines. So, as soon as possible after January 1, complete your income tax return (and your parents' return if you're a dependent). You do not have to *pay* your taxes before completing the FAFSA. You just need to fill out your return. It will make the FAFSA easier. If you have not completed your tax forms, estimate FAFSA information and correct it later. Then move on to the PROFILE if you need it.

The FAFSA asks about your finances and (if you're a dependent) your parents' finances. It asks for information you probably don't know without checking. Look at the FAFSA website. Ask your parent(s) to look at it, too. Information on the site is available in English and Spanish. Watch FAFSA videos on YouTube (youtube.com).

Start by looking at the guidelines for federal financial aid. You must be a US citizen. (There are very few exceptions.) You must have a social security number. If you are a man, 18 to 25 years old, you must register with the Selective Service. The **Selective Service** is a government agency that drafts men into military service if there is a national emergency and too few people join on their own. If you are not already registered, you can register online at sss.gov. To be eligible for federal financial aid, you also need to be working toward a degree, rather than just taking a few classes. The complete eligibility guidelines are on the studentaid.ed.gov website.

Next, decide if you should be completing your FAFSA application as a dependent or independent student. The government expects your parents to help pay for your college if they are financially able. You are an independent undergraduate college student if you are married, a military veteran, or are 24 or older on January 1 in the year you are starting college. If you are an orphan or ward of the court, you may also be independent. If you have children or other dependents and you provide more than 50 percent of their support, you may also be independent.

After you figure out if you should file as an independent or dependent student, start gathering information. You will need information for you, plus your parents (if you are a dependent student) and your spouse (if you're married). You'll need social security numbers, driver's license numbers, and W-2 forms. Employers send W-2 forms to employees in January. A **W-2** shows the amount the employee earned the previous year and the amount **withheld** (taken out) for taxes. You will also need information about SNAP (sometimes called food stamp) benefits from the past two years. You'll need last year's federal income tax returns and records about untaxed income. **Untaxed income** may include Temporary Assistance to Needy Families (TANF), welfare, social security and veteran's benefits. You'll also need information about child support paid or received. You'll need current bank statements and current business and farm records if you (or a parent) have a business or farm. You'll also need stock, bond, and other investment records.

Next, print a *FAFSA on the Web* worksheet from the FAFSA website. The worksheet will help you organize information and get ready to file. If you have a computer and internet access at home, it's a lot easier to file the FAFSA electronically. It's faster and includes error checks that help you avoid making mistakes or leaving out information. If you leave things out, it can slow down your application. The government can handle online applications more quickly. You can also check the status of the application online. You'll need to apply for a PIN at pin.ed.gov. A **PIN** is a personal identification number, like those for bank automated teller machines (ATMs). Your PIN allows access to your personal records. So, never give your PIN to anyone, and keep it in a safe place.

If you've already filed your federal tax return, you can use a tool from the Internal Revenue Service (IRS). The tool pulls information from the IRS for your online FAFSA. If you can use the IRS tool, it'll make the FAFSA easier. However, you cannot use the IRS method if you have not filed taxes yet or if you do not have to file taxes. If you use the IRS tool, make sure the information matches exactly. For example, if your father's first name is "Steven" on IRS forms, do not list it as "Steve" on the FAFSA.

You list colleges to which you are applying on the FAFSA. You can list up to ten schools. These schools will get your FAFSA results electronically. If you want to add or change schools later, you can make changes online with your PIN. You can also call the Federal Student Aid Information Center (1-800-433-3243).

GET HELP WITH THE FAFSA

Read the FAFSA instructions carefully. Errors and incomplete information will cause delays. If the FAFSA seems hard to complete, get some help. There are many tools to help you. Answers to frequently asked questions (FAQs) are on the website. You can also call 1-800-433-3243 (a toll-free number) or email questions through the website. The online application also has a "chat" feature, which allows you to ask questions as you complete the form.

The National Association of Student Financial Aid Administrators (NASFAA) provides good FAFSA advice. You can download tips from the student and parent section of the NASFAA website (nasfaa.org). High schools and colleges offer free workshops about financial aid and the FAFSA. If a workshop is available, ask a parent to go with you. If your parent cannot go, or doesn't want to, go alone. You will learn good information and meet people who can answer questions for you. Write down names and phone numbers of speakers so you will be able to contact them if needed.

College Goal Sunday workshops provide free help to complete the FAFSA. (Very few College Goal Sunday workshops are actually on Sundays. Most are on weekday evenings at high schools.) At these workshops, you complete the FAFSA with help from a professional. Check the collegegoalsundayusa.org website to see if there is a workshop in your area. (The "usa" in the website address is important. If you skip the "usa," you will get a site that just works for Indiana.) Read what to bring to the workshop. Bring the same information that you would need if you were completing the FAFSA at home.

You can also contact the financial aid office at a school where you're applying. The school may have people who can help you complete the FAFSA. Other non-profit groups will help, too. For example, the Iowa College Access Network (ICAN) has eight sites around the state. The professionals at those sites help families file FAFSAs. ICAN helps thousands of students each year – free! There are similar groups in many states.

FOLLOW UP ON THE FAFSA

So, what happens after you complete the FAFSA? First, the federal government conducts a **needs analysis**. It reviews information about your income and savings, your parents' income, and some of your family's **net assets** (cash, bank accounts, and investments minus loans and other debts). The needs analysis takes into account **family expenses** (based on income taxes, housing, clothing and food costs, number of family members, number in college, your parents' need to save for retirement, etc.) The needs analysis for federal or state aid does not include **home equity** (the value of your home minus any mortgage or home equity loan). However, colleges and scholarship agencies may consider home equity as they make decisions about their scholarships and grants.

Within a month (or sooner, if you file online) you will get a **Student Aid Report** (SAR). Your SAR will list your **Expected Family Contribution** (EFC). The EFC is a measure of your family's financial strength. Your EFC may not be the amount your family will pay for college. It is just a number used by schools to calculate the federal student aid you're eligible to receive.

If your application was incomplete, your SAR will not include an EFC. However, the SAR will tell you what to do next. When you get your SAR, review it carefully to make sure it is correct and complete. If you don't need any changes, just keep it for your records. If you find a mistake, you'll need to correct or update your FAFSA.

The schools you listed on your FAFSA use the Student Aid Report and FAFSA information to make decisions about federal and nonfederal need-based financial aid. A school may also ask you to verify (prove) the FAFSA information.

COMPLETE THE PROFILE, IF NEEDED

You should complete the PROFILE, if your target schools or scholarships need it, as soon as possible after the FAFSA. Complete it before the earliest school or scholarship priority deadline. Meet any priority deadlines. Colleges and scholarship agencies consider those who meet priority deadlines first. *If* they have any financial aid leftover, they *may* consider those who apply after the priority deadline.

About 400 colleges and scholarship agencies use the PROFILE. They list the PROFILE requirement in financial aid sections of their websites. The College Board (which manages the PROFILE) also lists schools and scholarship groups that need the PROFILE on its website, collegeboard.org. The PROFILE is not free like the FAFSA. However, schools that use the PROFILE have generous need-based financial aid. Therefore, it can definitely be worth your time and effort to complete it. In addition, low-income students get the PROFILE fee waived for up to eight colleges and scholarship agencies.

Complete the PROFILE online at student.collegeboard.org. Instructions are available in English and Spanish. Start by watching the online tutorial. The tutorial gives basic information and directs you to other sources of help if you have questions. After watching the tutorial, register for the PROFILE. When you register online, you'll list the schools and scholarship agencies where you want PROFILE information sent. Print out the customized *Pre-Application Worksheet* and *Application Instructions*. These will list the information you'll need in order to complete the PROFILE for the schools and scholarships you listed. You'll need the same information as for the FAFSA and more. The PROFILE application digs deeply into your family's finances.

Gather the information and fill out the pre-application worksheet. Then set aside about two hours of quiet, uninterrupted time to complete the PROFILE online. Check to make sure everything is accurate. You can't change it after you file it. You can add more schools or scholarship agencies, but you can't delete any. If you make an error in the information you provide, you have to correct it individually with each school or scholarship agency. So, make sure the information is accurate *before* you send it. You'll need to pay with a valid credit or debit card. However, low-income students will automatically receive a fee waiver that covers the price of the PROFILE registration and reports to up to eight schools and scholarship agencies.

After you file your PROFILE, you may need to send copies of federal tax returns and other information. If your parents are divorced, your **non-custodial parent** (the one you don't live with) will probably need to provide more information, too. After you make FAFSA and PROFILE applications, if there are any changes in your family circumstances or finances, tell schools.

If your financial circumstances change after you start college, you can ask for a mid-year review of your financial aid. For example, if a parent loses a job or your family has big medical expenses, you may be able to get more aid.

COMPLETE THE FAFSA AND PROFILE EVERY YEAR

Don't forget – you must reapply for need-based financial aid *every* year. Be sure you know what needs done. In addition, be careful to meet all deadlines. You have to resubmit updated information for the FAFSA for federal aid. And you must update the PROFILE each year, too. However, it gets easier after the first year. Keep your sign-in information in a secure place. When you sign in to your account the following year, some of the information will already be there.

Some students who get federal Pell grants for their first year of college don't complete the FAFSA the next year. Maybe they don't realize they can apply for Pell grants for up to twelve semesters of college. Or maybe they just forget. If you get need-based aid your first year, you'll probably get some in later years, too. If you did not get need-based aid in year one but have a different situation (for example, lower income or more family members in college) in later years, file the FAFSA (and PROFILE, if needed). With different financial circumstances, you may become eligible for need-based aid.

SUMMARY

Applying for need-based financial aid takes time and energy. Students who get federal grants must complete the FAFSA. If you want federal college loans, they also depend on the FAFSA. In addition, you need it for many other need-based scholarships and grants. To be eligible for individual college, university, or agency scholarships and grants, you may need to complete the PROFILE, too. Most people find it easiest to complete their tax forms and then complete the FAFSA and PROFILE as soon as possible. Provide complete and accurate information, and complete everything before priority deadlines.

Also, remember to file a new FAFSA (and PROFILE, if needed) for each year of college. Need-based grants and scholarships take work. But remember – it's free money!

CHAPTER 27 – COMPARE OFFERS, WEIGH OPTIONS, AND CHOOSE

After you apply for college admission and financial aid, get ready to wait. Students tell me it feels like their lives are on hold. It's tough to wait and see which colleges admit you and what they'll offer in financial aid.

The first message you'll get from a school is an admission decision. The school website tells you when to expect the decision and how it'll come (for example, by email or by letter). The message is usually straightforward, saying you're accepted or not. But it sometimes says you're **wait-listed**. This means you weren't accepted but you *might* get in if other students decide to go elsewhere.

It's tough to know what causes a school to prefer you to another student or vice versa. Often two people with similar test scores, activities, and high school records receive different admissions decisions. Sometimes it's as simple as one school having no other applicants from your state and another having too many. Few people get admission offers from every school where they apply. And many students decide, in the end, to attend a school that wasn't their first choice. According to the Higher Education Research Institute, about 75 percent of college freshmen get admission offers from their first choice schools. But only about 57 percent enroll there. Finances are the top reason students don't go to first-choice schools. Often they get more aid from other schools and decide those schools are better values.

Now, it's time to focus on schools that admit you. Then decide where to attend. If you're starting college in the fall, you'll need to focus on this decision during April. If you're accepted and applied for financial aid, you'll get a financial aid notice in early April. Detailed timelines are available on each college's website. Some schools send letters. Others send email notices. Others ask students to log into an online account to get the news. Most schools need you to accept or decline their offers by May 1. So, you have some serious thinking to do. And you only have about a month to do it.

Many colleges use a **shopping sheet**. The shopping sheet is a form, designed by the federal government, which shows financial aid information in a standard way. It makes it easier to compare information from different schools. A shopping sheet shows the costs of attending the college (for one academic year) and the aid you're eligible to receive. Other schools provide the same types of information, but on their own forms. So, you have to figure out how to compare the offers.

ANALYZE YOUR AWARD NOTICES

Gather your award notices. Make a copy of each, just in case you misplace one. Then begin a careful analysis. Wait to decide until you have notices from all schools. But you can start your analysis as soon as you get the first offer.

Start by reading each notice carefully. Make sure you understand all terms and conditions. Know if grants and scholarships are single-year or multiyear offers. Multiyear offers are renewable. The award letter applies *just* to the next school year, unless it says otherwise. This is a huge issue, so pay attention!

Many schools **front end** financial aid. This means they give more scholarship and grant aid in the first year, and less (or none) in later years. But you aren't planning to go to college for just one year. You need to think about how you'll pay for your entire college experience. For a bachelor's degree, this typically means at least four years.

One school might be offering a first-year $5000 scholarship. Another school might offer a $3000 scholarship that is renewable for three more years. At first glance, the $5000 scholarship looks better. But the $3000-a-year scholarship is worth $12,000 in total. So, look closely at whether scholarships and grants are single-year or multiple-year awards. Make sure you don't assume a scholarship or grant is renewable when it is a one-year award.

Know the conditions for multiyear awards. You must keep a minimum grade point average (GPA) and carry a minimum course load to keep most scholarships and grants. You sometimes have to keep a major or continue an activity. It's up to you to know and understand the rules for keeping your financial aid. Nobody keeps track of it for you. Your parents won't be getting your grades (even if they're paying a big part of costs). So, you can't rely on mom or dad to watch your financial aid.

If you've earned **outside grants or scholarships** (from a source other than the school), make sure you know how each school handles them. This can have a big impact on your net costs at different schools. Some colleges will reduce the loan portion of your package or the amount your family needs to contribute. Other schools reduce your Work-Study job by the amount of the outside scholarship.

Others may reduce **institutional** (the school's) aid. This is the *worst* way for a school to handle your outside scholarship because it gives you *no* benefit from the outside aid. If you have outside grants or scholarships, you want the college to use that money to reduce your family contribution or student loans. It's also OK to reduce your Work-Study, if you can find another job.

Offer letters may not spell out how schools treat outside scholarships. You may need to contact the financial aid offices to get answers to your questions. If you do, keep responses in your files. Pay careful attention to this. It can make a huge difference in your cost of college.

COMPARE NET PRICES

Once you understand offers, figure out your net price of one year at each school. Here's how to look at first-year costs:

A. Net tuition (tuition minus any discounts)

B. Net fees (fees minus any discounts)

C. Fixed costs (A + B)

D. Room charges

E. Board (meal plan or other food) charges

F. Travel between school and home

G. Estimated costs of books and supplies

H. Personal expenses

I. Other expenses (such as childcare, if applicable)

J. Flexible costs (D + E + F + G + H + I)

K. Total cost of attendance (C + J)

L. Institutional grants and scholarships from this school that that you don't have to repay (gift aid)

M. Federal Pell Grant

N. Federal Supplemental Educational Opportunity Grant

O. Other grants and scholarships that apply at this school, but not others (for example, a state grant that applies only at in-state schools)

P. Outside grants and scholarships you can accept without reducing institutional scholarships or grants (L)

Q. Total gift aid that does not require repayment or work (L + M + N + O+P)

R. Net price for one year (K-Q)

S. Work-Study/job offer

T. Federal Perkins Loan

U. Federal Direct Subsidized Loan

V. Federal Direct Unsubsidized Lo

W. Total federal student loan options–to be repaid, plus interest (T + U + V)

Before you go further, look carefully at the net price (R) of a single year at each school.

It's easy to compile this information in a Microsoft Excel spreadsheet, if you know how to use the program. You may also be able to use the online comparison tool at the Consumer Financial Protection Bureau. If schools send XML files of their award offers (and they use the standard Financial Aid Shopping Sheet), you can enter the XML codes online and compare the first-year financial aid offers. You'll find the tool at consumerfinance.gov/paying-for-college.

ESTIMATE YOUR TIME TO DEGREE AT EACH SCHOOL

Next, think about how long it would likely take to complete your degree at each school. Consider how long it takes most students to graduate at each school. Also, look at how much credit each school will grant from dual credit, AP tests, and other prior learning. Consider if any schools offer accelerated degree programs. Then make your best guess about how long it would take you to complete your bachelor's degree at each school.

ESTIMATE NET COST TO DEGREE AT EACH SCHOOL

Next, estimate the total net cost to get your degree at each school. We'll call this **net cost to degree**. For each school, multiply the first-year net price by the number of years you think it would take to complete your degree at that school. For example, let's assume that your net cost is $15,000 per year at College A, and you think it would take five years to get your degree there. The net cost to degree would be $75,000. College B might be offering $15,000 net cost for the first year, but $5000 of gift aid is not renewable. You'd need to increase the expected net price of later years to reflect the loss of this aid. The net price for any years beyond the first year would increase by $5000 per year.

By now, your head is probably spinning! The estimated net cost to degree may look huge. And it will likely end up worse than it looks right now. Prices will probably increase each year.

You'll probably see some big differences between schools. The net cost to degree at some schools may be less than expected. At others, it may be more. That's why it's so important to look at the net cost to degree. Net cost to degree is your best tool to compare costs of different schools and different options.

CONSIDER VALUE AND OTHER OPTIONS

It's time to start thinking seriously about value – the benefits you think you'd get from attending a school compared with the net cost to degree. At this point, students often drop some schools from consideration. The net costs may be too high when compared with the value.

It may also be time to think about transfer strategies. If you want to get your degree from one school, but the net cost to degree looks too high, can you start at a community college or in-state public and then transfer after two years? If you attend a community college, can you live with parents and not pay room and board? Or could you get your degree from a less expensive school and take classes at your dream school through an exchange, as discussed in Chapter 13?

You've probably now dropped some schools from consideration. But you likely have several choices that could make sense.

- One might be to attend a local community college for an associate degree and then transfer to a private that has an articulation agreement and transfer scholarships.
- A second might be to get a three-year accelerated bachelor's degree at a private college.
- A third might be to attend an in-state public school that offers an honors program and merit aid.
- A fourth might be to attend an out-of-state public that offers in-state tuition and AP credit.

Try to work though the numbers and decide which strategies make the most sense. Then estimate the total cost to degree for each strategy. Thinking about rewards and costs, some will look better than others will.

CONSIDER YOUR PAYMENT OPTIONS

The total net cost to degree may still look high. For most people, college is the biggest investment they'll ever make other than buying a house. But remember, there are many ways to pay for college. Most people pay from three types of income: past, present, and future. They may have some savings from past income. They'll also have student (and possibly parent) wages while in college. And they can take out student (and possibly parent) loans, which they'll pay back with future income.

Start by adding up the sources of money you already have available. Ideally, you have some savings you can use. Next, think about how much you can contribute from wages. For example, some schools may be offering Work-Study. Even if a school isn't offering Work-Study, you can probably get a job on or near campus. Add up the total amount that you and your parents can contribute from wages during your college years.

If you're a whiz at Microsoft Excel, you can complete a complex analysis here. If you know how, go for it! But most people do much simpler calculations. They just add up their savings and expected wages, and then subtract them from the total net cost to degree for each strategy. When you get down to the bottom line of how much you'd need to borrow for each scenario, you may drop some from consideration.

DECIDE HOW MUCH YOU'RE WILLING TO BORROW

Before you start thinking about *where* to borrow money, think seriously about *if* you want to borrow that much. Most financial advisors suggest students should never borrow more than the amount they can reasonably expect to earn their first year out of college. Do you know how much that is? Ideally, you have some idea from the career exploration you've done. If not, find out *before* you commit to loans.

Look at the Return on College Investment (ROCI) calculator on the Iowa Student Loan website (studentloan.org). It can help you understand the maximum amount of debt you can take on. Think through how much you can afford to borrow based on the career you're planning. Nobody has a crystal ball that can tell you what job you'll get and exactly what it'll pay. But you don't need to go into this blindly, either. You can also calculate how much your monthly loan payments would be. Use the calculator at finaid.org. Most experts recommend your monthly student loan payments be no more than 8 to 10 percent of your monthly wages.

MAKE SURE YOU HAVE THE BEST OFFERS

If the award package at your favorite school simply isn't enough, contact the financial aid office to be sure they aren't able to offer more aid. If your family's circumstances have changed or you have special circumstances, explain them. A special circumstance could be a job loss, divorce, salary decline, or death of a wage earner. It could also be high medical bills. Or there might have been one-time family events during the past year. Or the FAFSA might not fit your family's small business situation. If there are special circumstances, a financial aid director can use **professional judgment** to determine financial need.

Be cautious if you request a review of your award. Financial aid officers don't negotiate. Be professional and polite in your conversations. You're not haggling over the price of a used car! However, schools may match your offer from a similar school. Some schools, such as Harvard and Cornell Universities, are up front about their willingness to match offers for top students. But even schools that don't publicize a willingness to match offers often do. The school may be able to figure out a way to offer you more talent-based or merit grants or scholarships if you're outstanding in one or more areas. If you got a better package of grants and scholarships from a similar school, call the financial aid officer. Ask (politely) why the financial aid packages might be so different. Be very honest in your conversations about financial aid offers. Sometimes you'll need to provide copies of your offers from other schools. After you've made your case, wait to get final offers. Some schools wait until the last minute to make them.

DECIDE AND ACCEPT ADMISSION AND FINANCIAL AID

Once you have final offers, it's time to decide. Input from parents, friends, and others can be helpful. But in the end, the decision is yours. Consider all the information you've gathered and listen to your instincts. If two schools offer nearly identical costs and benefits, choose the more selective school. Students who attend schools that are more selective are more likely to complete their degrees than similar students who attend less selective schools.

Once you decide, accept. It's important to meet deadlines for enrolling and accepting financial aid. If you don't accept on time, the offer could go to another student. So, enroll and accept financial aid on time. And let schools you've decided against know, as well.

Read the next chapter before you commit to loans. Also, remember you *don't* have to accept the entire aid package exactly as offered. For example, some students decline Work-Study offers if they can get a better job off campus.

Send thank you notes to financial aid officers, especially those who've gone out of their way to answer questions and get you the most aid possible. A financial aid officer can be very helpful to you during college.

Pay deposits on time. Students normally have to pay a tuition deposit and a housing deposit. For most schools, you'll need medical forms completed. So, you may need to get a medical exam and **immunizations** (shots that protect you from common diseases) before you start classes. Students must also provide proof of current health insurance. Check to be sure that you've paid health insurance **premiums** (bills). Also, be sure to sign up for and attend orientation at the college you select.

REMEMBER THE RULES TO KEEP FINANCIAL AID

Remember what you must do to keep your financial aid beyond year one. You must reapply for need-based aid each year. Know the rules. Keep them in mind if you start thinking about dropping a class or falling behind. Nothing is more discouraging than to see a promising student get off track, lose his or her financial aid, and then drop out of school. I've had far too many students tell me after the fact, "I just didn't realize..."

SUMMARY

Compare financial aid offers from schools that accept you. Focus on the total net price to earn your degree. Remember, schools differ in the credit they award for prior learning. Some schools may offer accelerated degrees. And many grants and scholarships are just for the first year. Calculate the total net cost to complete your degree at each school. Do this for other scenarios, such as a community college for years one and two and a baccalaureate school for years three and four. Look for the best value – the best cost/benefit package for you.

Once you decide on the best plan, enroll, and accept the financial aid offer on time. And let the schools that you've decided against know, as well. Make sure you pay deposits and complete any other requirements on time.

Even if you're enrolling in a school that wasn't among your top choices, things have a way of working out. A 2014 study conducted by Gallup and the Lumina Foundation showed that business leaders say, "It's what you know, not where you go," when they hire. Another Gallup study released in mid-2014 suggests happiness after college depends more on what you *do* in school than which school you attend. I know many students who've had great experiences at colleges that weren't their top choices. Graduating from your second or third choice school with little debt may be a perfect launching point for a successful career and comfortable life!

CHAPTER 28 – BORROW AS LITTLE AS POSSIBLE

Many students have to borrow to finance college. Parents often borrow, too. The key is to borrow as little as possible, on the best terms, and keep your total debt at a manageable level.

The money a family pays for college comes from savings (past income), wages (present income), and loans (future income). When you estimated the total net cost to get your degree and compared that with your savings and wages, there was probably still a gap. Student and parent loans usually fill that gap.

When you looked at financial aid offers, you may have been surprised at how much you *could* borrow. You might have thought, "WOW – look at all the money I can get!" But hold on. Nobody is offering to *give* you that money. They're offering to *loan* you money. And you must pay back any money you borrow. Plus, you have to pay interest. You must repay your loans even if you don't finish your degree. You have to pay even if you can't find a job when you graduate.

BORROW ONLY WHAT YOU NEED

Your goal should be to borrow only what you absolutely need – not as much as you can. You *don't* have to borrow the amount of your loan offer. Take out a smaller loan if you don't need that much.

To get most types of loans, you need a steady job, a good credit rating, and collateral. A **credit rating** measures the chances you'll repay a debt. **Collateral** is something valuable you agree to give up if you don't repay a loan. For most types of loans, if you don't have a steady job, a good credit rating, and collateral, you must have co-signer who does. A **co-signer** agrees to pay back the loan if you don't.

It's easier to get federal student loans than other loans. You don't need to have a good credit rating. You don't need a job or other income. You don't have to own a house or car for collateral. And student loans don't need a co-signer.

Excessive loans can cause problems for decades. They have many people feeling handcuffed to jobs they don't like. They keep others from getting married, starting families, or buying cars and houses. If you get behind on payments, it can even be hard to rent an apartment or get a job.

A 2014 Gallup-Purdue study found that college graduates with high levels of student debt ($50,000 or more) face long-term challenges. The survey focused on five elements of well-being:

- *Purpose*: liking what you do each day and being motivated to achieve your goals
- *Social*: having supportive relationships and love in your life
- *Financial*: managing your economic life to reduce stress and increase security
- *Community*: liking where you live, feeling safe, and having pride in your community
- *Physical*: having good health and enough energy to get things done daily

You'd expect people with more student debt to have more financial challenges. But those with higher debt also experienced challenges in the purpose, community, and physical aspects of their lives. So, be smart about borrowing. Don't take on any more debt than you need. Borrow as little as possible, and on the best possible terms.

DEVELOP A BUDGET

Start by developing a budget to figure out how much you need to borrow. There are many online tools. The US Department of Education has some designed for college students. Search "college student budget calculator" at their website (ed.gov). You can use an online calculator, make a computer spreadsheet, or develop a budget by hand.

When a college lists its cost of attendance, the estimates are high. Some costs, like tuition and fees, are fixed. But many, such as books, room, board, and travel, are flexible. You can reduce these. For example, when colleges estimate room and board costs, they assume students will live in a double room on campus. And they assume students will buy full meal plans. But you may be able to live at home, or get a job that provides free room and board. (See Chapter 32 for more information.) Similarly, when colleges estimate the cost of books, they assume you will buy new books. But as you'll read in Chapter 33, you can save money on textbooks. Read these chapters (and others in Part Five) to find ways to cut flexible expenses.

As you develop your budget, think about cash flow. **Cash flow** is the movement of money. Think about when you'll get money and when you must pay bills. For example, you might start a job the same week you start classes. You have to pay tuition and fees for classes *before* they start. You pay room and board *before* you eat or sleep there. But you aren't paid for work until *after* you've done it. Some schools have payment plans, in which you can divide the payment rather than paying all bills up front. Most schools charge a fee for this service, but it can help cash flow. Also remember, if you live off campus, you'll need to pay deposits (apartment, electricity, water, etc.) and rent up front.

If you have scholarships, grants, and federal loans, they typically pay the school directly. The school then pays you any amount left after tuition and fees (and room and board, if you live in school housing). The school pays you at least once each term. When you start college, you normally have to wait about thirty days to get your first **disbursement** (payment).

UNDERSTAND STUDENT LOANS

Next, understand the language of loans. The money you borrow is the **principal**. You must repay it. You must also pay **interest**, the cost of borrowing money. The **interest rate** is a percentage of the amount you borrow. For example, if you borrowed $1000 at 4 percent annual interest, the fee would be $40.

Federal student loans have **fixed interest rates**. These stay the same for the life of the loan. Some loans have **variable interest rates**, which can go up or down. Most lenders charge **loan origination fees**. You pay this to **process** (set up) your loan. The lender sometimes takes the origination fee from the **proceeds** (money) they **disburse** (pay). If you borrow $1000 and have a 1 percent loan origination fee ($10), you might get a check for $990. But you owe $1000 (the principal), plus interest. Some lenders add the origination fee to the principal. In this case, you'd get a check for the full $1000. The principal would be $1010 and you'd pay 4 percent interest on $1010. So, you'd be charged $40.40 for the first year's interest.

Some federal loans don't charge interest while you're in school. Other loans do. You can sometimes **defer** (postpone) interest fees. If deferred, the lender **capitalizes** the interest (adds it to your loan principal). So, you pay interest on the original loan plus the deferred interest. Suppose, for example, you had a $1000 loan at 4 percent interest. If you defer interest and capitalize it, the principal after one year would be $1040. During the second year, you'd pay interest on $1040. If you deferred interest and capitalized it the next year, you'd owe $1081.60 at the end of year two. If you borrowed another $1000 during year two on the same terms, you'd owe $2121.60 at the end of year two. Many students don't realize how much it costs to defer payments. Deferred payments add up quickly. Pay attention.

Federal loans are available to US citizens who attend college at least half time. **Enrollment status** controls eligibility for some loans and loan amounts. **Full time** means twelve or more credits each term. **Half time** is six credits each term. The **repayment period** is the maximum time you have to repay your loan. The **grace period** is the time you have after you graduate (or drop below half-time enrollment) to start repaying your loan. As you're repaying, the amount you have left to pay is the **outstanding principal balance**. A **deferment** is the time a lender lets you postpone repaying all or part of your loan. You might get a deferment, for example, if you enroll in graduate school. Remember, a deferment just means you're postponing payment. You still have to repay the loan, plus any additional interest owed.

Student loans from the federal government usually have the best rates, terms, and consumer protections. (But federal loans don't all have the same rates and terms.) They are usually the only student loans that can be forgiven through government programs. (Read the next chapter to learn more about this.) If you are planning to work after graduation in a job that forgives your student loans, make sure you get the right kind of student loans.

The federal government, some states, and some schools offer need-based loans. The information you provide in the FAFSA determines whether you're eligible. Need-based loans are often subsidized. The government (or school) provides money so low-income students can borrow for college at lower interest rates. Lenders usually charge higher interest rates for unsubsidized loans. And you must usually repay unsubsidized loans sooner.

The federal government has two types of need-based loans. Students with the highest need get **Federal Perkins Loans**. These have the lowest interest rates and the most favorable terms. However, not all schools participate and, due to limited funds, not everyone who qualifies gets one. If you can get a

Perkins Loan, this should be the first loan you accept. The other federal need-based student loans are **Federal Direct Subsidized Loans**. These loans have subsidized interest rates and more favorable terms than most loans. If needed, this should be the second type of loan you take.

The federal government also offers unsubsidized college loans. **Federal Direct Unsubsidized Loans** are loans to students. Federal **Parent PLUS Loans** are for parents. Interest rates are higher than subsidized loans. Student loans have lower interest rates and lower loan origination fees than parent loans. Parent PLUS Loans consider a parent's credit history. A parent with an adverse (bad) credit history wouldn't normally get a Parent PLUS Loan. However, some parents with adverse credit histories can get Parent PLUS Loans if they have a qualified endorser. An **endorser** is someone who agrees to pay the loan if the parent doesn't.

Prepayment penalties are fees you must pay if you repay all or part of a loan early. Federal loans do not have them. There are also other consumer protections with federal loans. For example, federal student loans can sometimes be forgiven (cancelled) if you work in a public service job after graduation. (Read Chapter 29.) Some federal student loans have **income-based repayment** options. This means monthly payments depend on how much you earn. And there are opportunities to **consolidate** (combine) federal loans.

Learn details about federal loans at studentaid.ed.gov. You can log into this website using your FAFSA PIN number. You'll need to complete a course about federal student loans before you get any. But you can learn more now by looking at the studentaid.ed.gov website.

Be sure you understand the **terms** (conditions) of loans. It's important to know the interest rate, when interest charges begin **accruing** (building up), when you must start repaying the loan, and how long you have to repay it. It's important to understand the terms of any loan *before* you commit. Read and understand the fine print. President Obama tells students to "know before you owe!"

If you get a federal student loan, you must sign a **Master Promissory Note** (MPN). It's a contract that defines the conditions under which you're borrowing and agree to pay back the loan. A **loan servicer** collects payments on your loan and responds to questions. You repay a loan by making regular scheduled payments to the loan servicer. If you take out a loan, make sure you know the loan servicer. Pay attention to any correspondence you get from them.

CONSIDER OTHER PLACES TO BORROW

Other places loan money for college. Some don't charge high interest rates. For example, if you've decided to attend school in your home state, there may be state-subsidized college loans. If your parents have good credit ratings, jobs, and collateral, they may be able to get loans with better interest rates and terms than Parent PLUS Loans. Parents don't get the repayment options that students get for federal student loans. So, if a parent is going to borrow to help pay for college, consider options beyond Parent PLUS Loans.

Some tax-preferred retirement plans (such as IRAs, 401Ks, and 403Bs) let owners withdraw to pay education expenses. The downside is the money you take out isn't growing in value and set aside for retirement. Plus, you must be careful to follow rules exactly to avoid tax penalties. Some life insurance policies also let owners borrow against the cash value of the insurance. The downside is the insurer pays less if the person dies.

If you or your family owes little on a home mortgage, you may want to refinance to cover education expenses. A home equity loan is another possibility. An advantage is the interest may be tax deductible. The disadvantage is your parents (or you, if it's your house) would have larger payments. Plus, the house is collateral. So, you could lose the house if you can't repay on time.

You can also get **private student loans**. Non-government lenders (such as banks and credit unions) make these. Private loans often have higher interest rates and higher loan origination fees than federal loans. They also have less-flexible repayment options, fewer opportunities to be forgiven, and fewer consumer protections. For example, if you become unemployed, you can get federal student loans deferred. With a private loan, you usually don't have that option. Private loans also don't have flexible repayment options like federal loans. For example, you can't make payments based on your income.

KEEP TRACK OF YOUR LOANS

If you accept loans, keep track of them. Keep track of federal student loans at nslds.ed.gov. This is the site for the National Student Loan Data System (NSLDS). Once you graduate, look into a **consolidation loan**. This combines existing loans into one new loan. It could have better terms (interest rate, repayment timelines, monthly payments, etc.) than existing loans. However, you lose the consumer protections and repayment options of a federal loan if you consolidate it into a private loan. So, be careful.

SUMMARY

Many students borrow for college. It's a good investment if you finish college and you don't borrow too much. Most experts recommend your monthly student loan payments be no more than about 8 to 10 percent of your monthly income when you graduate.

Borrow as little as possible, and get the best deal. Before you commit to the loan, make sure you understand the terms. Federal subsidized loans are usually the best student loans. Non-subsidized federal loans also have some consumer protections and loan repayment plans that aren't available with private loans. Keep track of your loans. Remember, you must repay most loans if you ever drop below half-time enrollment. Be careful if you're considering dropping classes. Know how that decision could affect your scholarships, grants, and loans.

CHAPTER 29 – GET WORK-CONTINGENT MONEY

There are military and non-military public service jobs that can help with college costs. Some people call these **work-contingent financial aid** or **service scholarships**. You can repay all (or a portion) of your federal student loans with these programs. (Other loans don't usually qualify.) In exchange, you work in a particular job and location for a set time.

AMERICORPS

AmeriCorps is one of these programs. Members, including many recent college graduates, work in more than 2000 organizations across the country. These include non-profits, schools, and public agencies, plus community and faith-based groups. Job assignments depend on skills and interests as well as program needs. They include building affordable housing, teaching computer skills, working in after-school programs, and helping respond to disasters. Some AmeriCorps groups provide free college advice to low-income students.

Some students join AmeriCorps right out of high school. These students take a **gap year**, a year off between high school and college. Gap years are common in Europe. Students use them to help focus career goals so they're ready for college.

AmeriCorps' National Civilian Community Corps (NCCC) program is a ten-month, full-time experience for people 18 to 24. Projects are in partnership with non-profits, cities, states, the federal government, national and state parks, Indian tribes, and schools. Members work in teams of 8-12 people. They work on projects near Denver (Colorado), Sacramento (California), Perry Point (Maryland), Vicksburg (Mississippi), and Vinton (Iowa). Full-time members get a living allowance, healthcare, and childcare. When they complete their service, they get education grants. They can use awards to help pay for college or graduate school, or to pay student loans. Many schools match these grants for incoming students with extra scholarships or academic credits. Members who serve part time receive similar, but fewer, benefits. For more information about AmeriCorps, visit nationalservice.gov.

PROGRAMS FOR EDUCATORS AND ADVISORS

Teach for America is a nationwide program for recent college graduates. The program provides intensive teacher training and support. Some people join as certified teachers, but many have other majors. Members agree to teach for at least two years in a low-income school (preschool through twelfth grade). In return, they get a salary, health insurance, and retirement benefits. They may also get education benefits like AmeriCorps members. Learn more at teachforamerica.org.

The College Advising Corps is similar to Teach for America. Recent college graduates (from about 25 member colleges and many different majors) work with students in low-income schools and communities. They help students identify colleges and scholarships, and help complete applications. They receive a salary, health insurance, and training, plus an education award to repay student loans or future education expenses. Learn more at advisingcorps.org.

TEACH grants from the US Department of Education provide up to $4000 a year to students who plan to teach. To receive the grant, you agree to serve in a high-need field at an elementary school, secondary school, or educational agency that serves low-income students. You also agree you'll teach for at least four academic years within eight years after getting your degree. If you don't complete your contract, your grant converts to a direct, unsubsidized loan. You must then repay the loan, with interest charged from the date the grant was paid. Learn more at studentaid.ed.gov.

The Public Service Loan Forgiveness Program (PSLFP) is another national program. It's set up to encourage people to enter (and stay in) full-time public service jobs. Former students qualify for forgiveness of the balance of direct student loans. This happens after they've made ten years of on-time, full payments while working for a public service employer. Qualifying jobs are with federal, state, and local government agencies or non-profit groups. Public education, public libraries, school libraries, and other school-based services qualify. Private non-profit employers sometimes qualify. But remember, you have to make on-time loan payments every month for ten years before this program forgives *any* remaining loan balances. Learn more at studentaid.ed.gov.

PROGRAMS FOR HEALTHCARE CAREERS

The National Institutes of Health (NIH) programs focus on professional degrees (such as medical doctor, nurse practitioner, or dentist). Some undergraduate funds are also available. NIH undergraduate scholarships pay up to $20,000 per year. These pay college expenses of low-income biomedical or health sciences students. If you get one of these scholarships, you must work (for pay) for NIH. You work ten weeks in the summer, plus one year (after graduation) for each year of your scholarship. Visit training.nih.gov/programs to learn more.

National Health Service Corps (NHSC) has many opportunities, especially if you're fluent in Spanish. If you get an NHSC scholarship, you agree to practice in a high-need community after graduation. The scholarship pays for your tuition, fees, books, supplies, and equipment. You also get a monthly stipend (allowance) to help with living expenses. To be eligible, you must be a US citizen enrolled in an accredited US healthcare program. You must be studying to become a medical doctor, nurse practitioner, nurse-midwife, physician assistant, or dentist. If you're an MD, you must complete your residency in Family Medicine, General Pediatrics, General Internal Medicine, Obstetrics, Gynecology, or Psychiatry. Once you've completed education and training, you choose where you'll serve from a list of NHSC-approved sites in high-need communities. You serve one year for each year of support you receive, with a two-year minimum. These positions pay competitive salaries. You can also apply for the NHSC Loan Repayment Program that repays up to $25,000 in loans for each extra year you serve. If you're interested in healthcare in a rural or inner-city area, it's a great deal!

I know a young woman who took advantage of these programs. She attended a private college for her undergraduate degree in biology and Spanish. She then trained to become a physician assistant at one of the country's top schools. Now, just fifteen years after starting college, she has a job she loves and that pays very well. Plus, she's debt free at 33! For more information about National Health Service Corps opportunities, visit nhsc.hrsa.gov.

STATE AND LOCAL PROGRAMS

There are many state and local programs that help repay college loans if you work in a critical profession. Some programs also offer housing. There are many for educators and healthcare professionals. A few are available for computer science, engineering, and veterinary medicine graduates. You must agree to work in a specific location. Your college or university financial aid and job placement offices are good places to learn about these opportunities.

SUMMARY

If you know you want to teach or work in healthcare or education and are willing to work in a specific location, you may qualify for programs that help pay for school or pay back student loans. However, even if they are "scholarships," these programs work more like loans. For the loan to be forgiven (cancelled), you have to hold up your end of the bargain. If for some reason you can't (or change your mind and don't want to) meet your obligations, you have to repay the loan and interest. Read the fine print. Make sure you're willing to uphold your end of the contract *before* you sign it.

CHAPTER 30 – GET
HEALTH INSURANCE

Do you have health insurance? Even if you've always been healthy and have never had a broken bone, you need health insurance. If you don't have health insurance, one car accident or serious illness could ruin your college plans.

In some states, students must prove they have health insurance before enrolling in college. You'll also get a federal tax penalty if you don't have health insurance. So, get it!

If you're under 26, the least expensive health insurance may be a parent's plan. Your parent's plan must cover you until you're 26, even if you're married and independent. If you're going to school in a different state, find nearby in-network providers. **In-network providers** are healthcare sources (such as hospitals and doctors) that your insurance company has approved. When you use these sources for healthcare, you get the lowest cost coverage. **Out-of-network providers** cost more.

An employer's plan may also cover you. Most employers pay a portion of the cost for full-time employees. Some employers offer health insurance to part-timers, too. Check with your human resources department.

If you need to find your own health insurance, see what's available through the Online Health Insurance Marketplace (healthcare.gov). Some states have their own health insurance **marketplaces** (sometimes called **exchanges**). The marketplaces help you locate and compare plans. They help you compare coverage, benefits, and premiums (fees). You can compare **deductibles** (the amounts you pay before the insurance pays) and **co-payments** (the amounts you pay for specific services, such as doctor visits or prescriptions).

Based on your income, you may be eligible for Medicaid. **Medicaid** is a US government-sponsored program that provides free or low-cost health insurance for low-income individuals and families. Based on your income, you might be eligible for tax credits that pay up front to help buy health insurance. These tax credits apply even for people who owe no federal income tax. But the tax credits only work for insurance bought through a health insurance exchange. Student health insurance plans are not eligible.

Figure out your alternatives for healthcare insurance. Compare rates and coverage to choose the best plan. But make sure you have healthcare insurance. Submit college health insurance forms on time. If you don't prove you have health insurance, some schools will bill you for student health insurance. Also, take a copy of your healthcare insurance card to college, and carry it with you.

Many college students have unhealthy lifestyles. Don't be one of them. Exercise regularly, get adequate sleep, eat a well-balanced diet, and don't drink excessive amounts of alcohol. If you're sexually active, practice safe sex. Many student health centers distribute free condoms. Planned Parenthood offers confidential, low-cost birth control options, too.

If you smoke, quit! Smoking is very expensive and creates major health risks. Most health insurance plans pay to help you stop smoking. Don't sunbathe, and use sunscreen when outdoors. There is no such thing as a "healthy tan."

SUMMARY

Get health insurance. If you don't have insurance though a parent's or employer's plan, look for coverage through the Online Health Insurance Marketplace. If your school requires students to carry health insurance, make sure you file the correct forms by the deadline.

Live a healthy lifestyle, so you stay healthy.

CHAPTER 31 – GET A JOB

Will you work while in college? Should you work full time or part time?

If you're like most students, you'll work while in college. According to the US census, about seven of every ten students work while earning their undergrad degrees. And about 20 percent of those who work hold full-time jobs.

According to the experts cited in *Understanding the Working College Student: New Research and Its Implications for Policy and Practice*, students who work ten to fifteen hours each week have better time-management skills and get better grades than those who don't work. But full-time students who work more hours often report negative effects on grades and the quality of their education. So, don't sacrifice the quality of your education trying to pay for it! And don't forget, scholarships and grants require you make progress toward your degree and keep a minimum grade point average (GPA). A job with flexible hours, which you can alter with your schedule, assignments, and exams, is ideal.

WORK-STUDY AND OTHER ON-CAMPUS JOBS

Start by considering Work-Study jobs. Most colleges and universities take part in the federal Work-Study program. Work-Study is a part-time employment program for US citizens (and permanent residents) who are at least half-time college students. School financial aid offices usually manage Work-Study programs. Eligibility and the maximum amount you can earn depend on your financial need as determined by the FAFSA. If you want a Work-Study job, apply early. Schools usually fill Work-Study jobs on a first-come, first-served basis.

Work-Study usually involves ten to fifteen (with a maximum of twenty) hours each week. Schools consider your class schedule and major when assigning jobs. Work-Study students earn at least the federal minimum wage. The wage rate for some jobs is higher because of the skills needed. For example, jobs that need computer programming or website development skills may pay higher wages. Work-Study jobs are normally on campus. However, they can be off campus with a non-profit organization or public agency.

One advantage of Work-Study jobs is that wages don't count as income on the FAFSA. You have report Work-Study wages, but they don't count against you. Wages from other jobs *do* count as income on the FAFSA. You must pay federal, state, and sometimes city income taxes on any wages, including those from Work-Study.

On-campus jobs have many advantages. You don't need transportation. You also don't waste time getting to and from work. And work schedules for on-campus jobs may be more flexible than other jobs. However, if you aren't eligible for Work-Study and don't have high-demand skills, you may have trouble finding an on-campus job.

The financial aid office usually manages Work-Study. Some schools have Student Employment Offices or websites to help students find other jobs. These are sometimes part of career services. To learn more about on-campus jobs, look on school websites under "Work-Study" and "student employment."

TAS AND RAS

Teaching and research assistantships are usually for graduate students. But exceptional undergrad students sometimes get these jobs. **Teaching assistants** (**TAs**) help professors with classes. They might run lab sections, post lectures online, monitor tests, or grade quizzes. **Research assistants** (**RAs**) help professors with research. They might run experiments, collect data, or analyze data. These jobs are sometimes Work-Study jobs. But they pay better than most. If your school offers you a teaching or research assistantship, you should probably accept it, especially if you're considering getting an advanced degree.

Most colleges hire mature third- and fourth-year students as **resident advisors (RAs)** for dormitories. RAs typically get free housing. They sometimes get a small salary or free meals, too. If you're interested in a career in teaching, higher education administration, or counseling, you might find this part-time job both educational and rewarding. (See the next chapter for more information.)

OFF-CAMPUS JOBS

Work-Study jobs are convenient. But if you have in-demand skills and can find another job nearby, it might pay better. Some off-campus jobs have good benefits for students, too. Some employers pay a portion of tuition for part-timers, to reduce turnover. Some even offer health and life insurance. This can be a great benefit, especially if you have a spouse or children that your plan will cover. Ideally, you can find a job that matches your career interests.

I met a young man who took computer classes at a community college while in high school. He learned other programming in online courses. He earned certifications in several computer specialties before he started college. He was then able to earn nearly $40 per hour as a programmer during college.

Another man I know majored in hotel and restaurant management. He worked weekends as a waiter at an expensive restaurant. His wages were low but, with his knowledge of food, friendly personality, and attention to detail, he earned excellent tips. He also got many free meals. Plus, he got valuable experience and had several great job offers when he graduated.

If you're considering a career in teaching, one of the best part-time jobs is tutoring. If you're a strong student and a good communicator, there are many tutoring opportunities. Tutoring has flexible hours and can increase your own understanding of a subject. After doing well in several undergrad accounting classes, my daughter tutored students in introductory classes. Today, she's an accounting professor.

If you excel in a sport or on an instrument, you might teach private lessons. One of my friends was a lifeguard. She taught private swimming lessons in college. She also got free access to a pool and recreation center. I know another young woman who taught piano lessons. She was getting her degree in music education, so it was a terrific part-time job.

While in college, I worked some evenings as a receptionist. I was busy during early evening hours. But later, there were few guests or phone calls. I had to stay at the desk in case anyone called or stopped by. But I wasn't busy, so my supervisor suggested I spend the time studying. They paid me to study!

Earn Extra Money

Babysitting, pet sitting, and housesitting are good ways to earn extra money. I did them all. The student employment office kept a list of students available to babysit. The pet and housesitting jobs came through professors and the dean's office. None of these jobs paid a lot. But they paid enough to be worthwhile.

If you're looking to pick up extra spending money, sign up for research studies. Business schools and psychology departments at research universities are always looking for **subjects** (people who take part in studies). Look for announcements on bulletin boards and student websites. It's a good way to pick up $10 or $15.

Universities with medical centers often need people to participate in clinical research. Researchers pay healthy people to participate. If you're considering a medical career, it might also be interesting. Just be sure to fully understand and consider any risks before participating.

There are often plasma centers near campuses. Many students earn extra cash selling their plasma (the colorless, fluid part of blood). Be careful to follow rules about how often you have plasma drawn. And follow any other instructions. Your health is important!

WORK DURING WINTER BREAK

Most colleges have a winter break in December and January. See if you can work at a retail store during this busy time. My son worked at a retail store during high school. He was able to work there again during college breaks. The store needed help with holiday sales and inventory. It was a great way to pick up extra cash. He also saw friends and got employee discounts on holiday presents. Plus, he developed skills useful in his marketing career.

CONSIDER WORKING FULL TIME

Some students work full time while in college. It takes time-management skills and energy. Some even manage a full course load while working full time. If you're going to try this, look for a program for working adults that provides support services. (See Chapter 9 for more information.)

I've known people who earned an associate degree and then worked full time. They used employer education benefits to finish bachelor's degrees. One person got an associate degree in computer science and then got his BS in computer engineering at night. Another got an associate degree in architectural drafting. He worked as a draftsperson while getting his BA in architecture. Another woman got her associate degree in nursing and then finished her bachelor's degree part time. She used this same strategy to earn an advanced degree, too.

Disciplined, energetic, long-range thinkers do well with this strategy. They have solid careers and little or no student debt.

There are many advantages of working full time while going to college. You have income, and often health and life insurance, paid mostly by your employer. And, your employer will often pay for some education expenses. Review Chapter 20 for more information about employer education programs.

SUMMARY

Working can help you avoid going deeply into debt to pay for college. Work-Study jobs have some distinct advantages, but may pay less than off-campus jobs. Try to find a job where you'll learn new skills and earn good wages at the same time.

Disciplined, energetic, long-range thinkers may want to earn all or part of their degree while working full time at an organization that provides education benefits.

CHAPTER 32 – FIND
LOW-COST ROOM AND BOARD

Where will you live while in college? Can you save money living somewhere else?

The price of living and eating on campus for four (or more) years can be a big part of college costs. Typically, room and board costs about $5000 each semester, with extra charges for single rooms and more complete meal plans. Some schools require students to live on campus. But even if you live on campus, you can trim room and board expenses.

LIVE AT HOME

Few older adults move to earn an undergraduate degree. But there are exceptions. Some people want to start over and move to a new place. Others need to move to get a specific major. And some adults, like veterans leaving the service, already need to move. So, they move to a place with a great college or university. However, most adults attend college without moving to a new location. They have housing and meal expenses, but they aren't higher than before college.

The best way for younger students to trim expenses is to live with a parent or other relative who doesn't charge rent. I saved a lot during internships and student teaching by living with relatives who let me stay rent-free in a spare bedroom.

About half of today's single undergrads live with their families. Community college students and urban students often live at home. If you don't have to pay rent and can commute to campus using public transportation, you can save several thousand dollars each year. But if you live at home, become involved on campus through clubs, sports, or other activities.

Some universities have special clubs to get commuter students active in campus life.

Talk with your parent(s) about the rules and responsibilities of living at home. Everyone needs to agree on what will (and won't) change as you become a college student living at home.

Look at Lower-Cost Dorm and Dining Options

Sometimes students can't live at home. The school you choose may be too far away. Or your family home might be unstable. There are still ways to save on housing and meals. Some colleges offer only full-meal plans, which cover 20 or more meals each week. Others offer many plans. Normally, a full-meal plan has the lowest price per meal. But it doesn't make sense to pay for meals if you're not going to eat them. For example, if you rarely eat breakfast or just have a bagel and juice, see if there's a no-breakfast plan. And if you have a job that provides free meals, don't pay for them at school.

Most schools quote room and board prices based on double rooms. But there may be lower-cost options. For example, **quads** (four students sharing a bedroom) have lower rates than double rooms. Older dorms and dorms without conveniences, like air conditioning, often cost less. Ask the housing office if there are lower-cost options.

Work For Your Room and Board

Sometimes you can work in exchange for housing or meals. Schools have student employment websites or offices that can help you find these jobs, on and off campus.

I've known many students who worked for room and board. Every person was glad he or she did. Each got more than money from the experience. Most enjoyed lifelong friendships with their employers. For example, I know a man who did yard work, snow removal, and driving for an elderly couple while in college. He got free room and board (his own bedroom and bathroom, plus home-cooked meals). He stayed in touch with the couple long after he graduated.

I know professors who employ education students as nannies. Students live with the families, take care of children while professors are on campus, and even have cars to drive. Some of these people (men and women) take full class schedules, yet earn their room and board, plus a salary. And they gain good work experience, too.

People interested in healthcare or social service careers may also find good jobs that include free room and board. Domestic violence shelters, assisted living facilities, and disabled individuals often hire people to help nights and weekends.

I knew a wealthy widow who lived in a university town and employed four caregivers. With their help, she lived in her own home. The overnight and weekend employees lived there, too. They each had a private bedroom and bathroom. They were full-time students working on nursing degrees.

People who work these types of jobs may not get a full night's sleep every night. But free housing and meals often come with the job. Plus, they get salaries and valuable career experiences.

BECOME A RESIDENT ADVISOR

Think about applying to become a resident advisor (RA). You get free housing. Some also get a small salary or free meals. An RA typically lives in a single dormitory room and is responsible for supervising nearby students. RAs enforce rules, provide guidance to other students, resolve conflicts, coordinate activities, and handle emergencies. Resident advisors are usually third- or fourth- year students who display leadership, responsibility, maturity, and respect for individual differences. It's a great way to cut college costs and gain valuable experience at the same time.

WORK IN FOOD SERVICE

There are also many opportunities in food service. University dining halls, sororities, fraternities, and restaurants (on and off campus) need workers. And most provide free or reduced-price meals and wages. My college boyfriend (now my husband) worked in food service. Even now, he sometimes mentions the extra helpings of favorite foods that were a bonus with his jobs.

CONSIDER A HOUSING COOPERATIVE

Housing cooperatives (also called **co-ops**) may provide another affordable alternative. In a housing cooperative, members jointly own houses or apartment buildings. Members control how the co-op runs. You usually get your own bedroom and share the bathrooms, living room, kitchen, and other common spaces with other members. Many cooperatives also share meals. Each co-op member has duties, such as cleaning, yard work, or maintenance. You pay to join the cooperative, plus a monthly fee to cover expenses such as property taxes, insurance, water, heat, and electricity.

Cooperatives are common in some parts of the country, especially in urban areas. Cooperatives are common in New York City, Chicago, Miami, Minneapolis, Detroit, Atlanta, San Francisco, and Washington, DC. But there are also cooperatives in smaller cities. For example, the Student Housing Cooperative at Michigan State University (msu.coop) provides low-cost housing in Lansing, Michigan. More than 200 member-owners live in fifteen houses.

To find a cooperative, search the Internet for "student housing cooperatives in (city)." Also, check with the local board of housing. Some colleges keep lists of housing cooperatives that are looking for new members. People I know who've lived in housing cooperatives saved money. They also enjoyed living with a group of people. They made friendships, and some even married fellow co-op members.

CONSIDER APPLYING FOR SUBSIDIZED HOUSING

Many students qualify for government-subsidized low-income housing. It provides housing for people who can't afford market rates. The rent you pay depends on your income compared with average incomes in the area. Public housing comes in all sizes and types, from single-family houses to high-rise apartments. People often imagine crime-infested public housing projects. But there is often nice public housing near campus. If you qualify, the government makes payments to the property owner, so you pay less rent.

If you think you might qualify, contact the local public housing agency where you'll attend college. Contact them as early as possible. You'll likely start on a waiting list. To find out how to contact your local agency, check hud.gov.

CONSIDER APPLYING FOR NUTRITION ASSISTANCE

Many college students also qualify for the Supplemental Nutrition Assistance Program (SNAP, sometimes called food stamps). If you qualify, you get an Electronic Benefits Transfer (EBT) card. It works like a debit card. When you buy groceries, you swipe the card and your benefit balance reduces by the cost of your groceries. The card supplies buying power each month based on family size and income. You can buy almost any food, except for deli items, hot foods, and alcohol. The US Department of Agriculture (USDA) website (usda.gov) has links to each state. If it looks like you'll qualify, contact the local food assistance office.

Many people need public housing and food assistance. Some are elderly, homeless, or disabled. So, if you don't really need it, don't apply. Leave the opportunity to someone who does – possibly another person reading this book right now.

GET YOUR PARENTS TO BUY A HOUSE OR CONDO

If your parents have money to invest, they might consider buying a house or condominium and then renting it to you. I know one family who had three sons headed to the same school. They bought a house and let each son be the landlord as he went through college. The sons found renters, collected rent, mowed grass, shoveled snow, and unclogged toilets. The parents **wrote off** (claimed) many expenses on income taxes. And they sold the house at a profit when the last son graduated.

Another family has a son who attended the same university for undergrad and dental school. The parents bought a condominium. The parents wrote off loan interest, property taxes, and other expenses while renting to their son. When he graduated from dental school, they sold the condominium. Most families can't make these kinds of investments. But if yours can, it's worth considering.

SUMMARY

Room and board expenses can easily top $40,000 during college. Look for ways to lower, or even eliminate, these expenses. Consider commuting, working for room and board, living in a housing cooperative, or living in low-cost public housing.

CHAPTER 33 – SAVE
A BUNDLE ON BOOKS

College students are surprised at the cost of textbooks. And parents are stunned! We're all used to buying books for $25 or less. So, when we see a textbook that costs $150 – or more – it's a shock.

According to the College Board, the average college student needed to budget about $1250 for textbooks and supplies for the 2014-2015 school year. So, you could spend $5000 – or more – on textbooks for your undergraduate degree. However, there <u>are</u> ways to save.

BUY USED TEXTBOOKS

For many courses, you can buy used textbooks. The lowest-cost way is to buy directly from other students. Check out bulletin boards in the library, class buildings, dorms, and student lounges. If there's a student organization for your college or major, see if it sponsors a book exchange. You can also buy used books from local bookstores.

In many subjects, you can use an earlier edition of the textbook. I wouldn't recommend it for technology courses or fast-changing topics like Social Media Marketing. However, a textbook for courses like The History of Western Civilization or Advanced Calculus won't change much between editions. Check with professors about using earlier editions of books.

When I teach, I tell students if an earlier edition will work. Local bookstores probably won't have earlier editions, but you can usually find them online. If you decide to use an earlier edition, double-check assignments. Chapter 11 in the current edition might be Chapter 10 in an older book. Also remember, at the end of class you won't sell an older edition for as much as a current one.

BUY BOOKS ONLINE

You can also buy new and used textbooks online. Online sites may own the books or merely serve as a place for buyers and sellers to meet. Sites include:

- Amazon.com
- Barnesandnoble.com
- Chegg.com
- Half.com
- Directtextbook.com
- Textbook.com
- Addall.com
- Campusbooks.com
- Gettextbooks.com
- Valorebooks.com
- Cheapesttextbooks.com

Many textbooks are less expensive (even with shipping charges) when ordered online. If your order is large (or you have a coupon code), you can often get free shipping. Watch bulletin boards and the college newspaper for coupons. Buying used textbooks online and then reselling them to other students or online is a cost-effective way to handle textbooks.

If you order online, order early, so books arrive before classes start. Many online providers ship with US Postal Service media mail rates. Media mail rates are lower, but it is slower. If you order later, you may pay higher shipping costs to get your books in time for classes.

Sometimes books on foreign websites cost much less than US-based online stores. The re-imported price may even be less for books printed in the US. Compare prices (including tax and shipping) among sources. Then consider cost and convenience.

If you order online, be sure you order the exact book you need, that it's in stock, and that it'll ship quickly. A book that arrives a month after classes start is no bargain.

ONLY BUY WHAT YOU'LL USE

Publishers often **bundle** (package) the textbook with other add-ons (such as CDs, software, workbooks, study guides, and passwords for websites). The bundled price is less than buying parts separately. And these materials may help you learn. So, if you will use them, buy the bundle. But the price is higher than the textbook alone. And you can't resell some parts, such as software and passwords. So, don't buy the bundle unless you need it and will use it. If you don't need add-ons, try to buy the textbook alone.

RENT, BORROW, OR SHARE BOOKS

See if there is a book rental option on or near campus. Some colleges, departments, bookstores, and libraries rent books. Some schools, such as Northwest Missouri State University in Maryville, include textbook rental in standard fees. Students pay somewhat higher standard fees, but pay nothing more for textbooks. There are also some online book rental sites (including some booksellers listed on the previous page). Other rental sites include:

- Campusbookrentals.com
- Packbackbooks.com
- Bookrenter.com
- Knetbooks.com
- Textbookrentals.com

You may be able to read textbooks at the library. For most courses, professors put textbooks **on reserve** in the college library. This means you can only check the book out for a few hours and can't take it outside the library. Sometimes you can check reserve books out overnight right before the library closes. Other than the nights before exams, you'll probably be able to read textbooks at the library. You can photocopy pages with complex tables or diagrams, if needed.

You may also get help from a librarian. You can sometimes borrow textbooks at public libraries. Many libraries let you to keep the book longer if nobody is waiting for it. Use the library in the college town or your hometown. Where I live, I can borrow from six public libraries – at no charge! Each library has an online catalog and I can borrow ebooks without even going there. It's amazing what I can borrow at no cost.

One time I had to read fourteen books for an ethics course. It would've broken my budget to buy them. But a local librarian rescued me. I borrowed several books from the local library, and she ordered the rest through interlibrary loan. I paid nothing instead of several hundred dollars.

Some students share textbooks to cut costs. It requires cooperation and planning. But if you have a friend or dorm-mate in the same class, try it.

LOOK FOR EBOOKS

Your textbook may be available as an ebook from many sites, including:

- eBooks.com
- Anyschool.com
- Amazon.com
- Googleplay.com
- Individual textbook publishers

You can buy ebooks. You can also rent some ebooks for the length of the course.

You may also want to look into Amazon Student services. The annual membership fee includes free shipping from Amazon and free borrowing rights for Kindle e-books. There is also a free app, so you can read Kindle books on other devices (a computer, tablet, smartphone, etc.)

The best ebooks to buy are for technology classes. Content in some technology fields changes so quickly you can't buy or sell used textbooks. So, for technology classes, buying or renting an ebook may be a great choice.

A few of your textbooks may even be free online from sources like:

- The Internet Archive (archive.org
- Project Gutenberg (gutenberg.org)
- Manybooks.net

Free ebooks are mostly in literature, English, math, history, and other fields that don't change quickly. If you're lucky, you'll have some professors who use these tools.

Some schools are working to develop textbook-free classes – and even textbook-free degrees. They use **open educational resources** (OER). These materials are usually online and are available free for learning, assessment, and research. For example, Tidewater Community College in Virginia offers an associate degree in business administration for which students buy no textbooks. Professors use open educational resources.

RETURN OR SELL WHAT YOU DON'T NEED

If you decide to switch a class, you need to be able to return the book and get a refund. So, if you think you might drop a class, don't buy from an online seller that doesn't accept returns. Don't open any bundles of materials until you're sure you need all parts. Keep sales receipts and the original packaging.

If you don't need a book for future reference, sell it after the course. And sell it quickly. If you wait a couple semesters, professors will be using a later edition, and you may not find a buyer. You'll get the best price if you sell the book directly to another student. Some schools or departmental clubs coordinate book exchanges. Or post an ad on bulletin boards on campus. I remember one creative student who walked around on the first day of classes holding a sign that read, "Textbooks for Sale – CHEAP."

You can also sell books online without much work at sites like Half.com. You list the book by ISBN number and condition. (The **ISBN number** is the **International Standard Book Number**. Look on the second page of a book, right behind the title page.) The website tells you prices of similar books, so you know how much to ask. Once the book sells, you get a message telling you where to ship it. Then you mail the book (using low cost media mail). Buyers pay through sites like Paypal.com. Bookstores also buy used books. However, they need to make a profit, so they may not pay as much you'd get selling the book directly to another student.

SUMMARY

College students can spend $5000 or more on textbooks while earning a bachelor's degree. But by planning and being creative, you can save a bundle on textbooks. Borrow or share books. Buy only the books and other materials that you need and will use. Buy used or ebooks when possible, and shop around for the best prices.

CHAPTER 34 – GET A BANK ACCOUNT, BUT SKIP CREDIT CARDS

Do you need a bank account in your college town? What about credit cards?

There are whole books written about student banking and credit card debt. We'll just cover the basics here. As a law professor I know tells students, "If you live like a lawyer when you're a student, you'll live like a student when you're a lawyer."

You may need a local bank account. That way you can use the bank's ATMs (automatic teller machines) without **withdrawal fees** (charges to take money out of your account). Find a bank or credit union that has ATMs on or near campus and doesn't charge ATM fees. Avoid overdraft fees by tracking spending and account balances. Set up free e-alerts to let you know if your balance is low.

Look for a bank that has low fees. Many banks and credit unions in college towns have special accounts for students. These usually have reasonable fees and features that are popular with students.

You can often avoid fees by signing up for a monthly direct deposit (for example, from your job or a parent). My husband and I scheduled monthly direct deposits to each of our college students' accounts. It was just enough so they wouldn't have to pay.

Avoid check printing costs by paying bills online or using a debit card. A **debit card** takes money from your account as soon as you use it. Banks usually provide them at no charge.

Be cautious about credit cards. Don't let handsome guys and cute coeds offering free water bottles or T-shirts lure you into credit cards. Credit cards spell trouble for college students. Sales pitches say you need a credit card to **establish** (build) your credit. That's nonsense. When you graduate and get a full-time job, you'll have time to establish credit.

With credit cards, it's easy to spend more money than you have. And bills, interest charges, and late fees add up. Students who rack up credit card debt establish a credit history – a bad one. It's much better to have *no* credit history than to have a *bad* credit history!

Our children argued they needed credit cards for emergencies. Since they were often halfway across the country, we decided they were right. So, we let them have a credit card on our account. But it came with a strict rule: it was only for emergencies. Occasionally, we let them use the card for something else. For example, they invited a friend and charged a nice dinner on their birthdays. It was a welcome treat within the rules.

When you're about to graduate and have a job lined up, get a credit card. Compare terms at sites like creditcards.com or nerdwallet.com. Think about how you'll use the card. Compare annual fees, interest rates, payment terms, and late fees. If possible, find a card with no annual fees and a long **grace period** (the time before interest starts accumulating). Then, pay your complete bill on time, every month, so you never pay late fees or interest charges.

SUMMARY

Get a checking account in your college town. Find a bank or credit union that has ATMs on or near campus and doesn't charge fees. Skip credit cards until you're ready to graduate. Then find one with no annual fees and a long grace period. Use it responsibly. Pay your full bill on time, every month.

CHAPTER 35 – DITCH THE CAR

Do you need a car at college? If you've had access to a car, the thought of being without one is uncomfortable. But unless you're commuting and there's no public transportation, having a car at college is a waste of money.

If you take a car to school, you'll probably have to pay to park it. And your assigned parking may be miles from your dorm. So, you'll either waste time getting to and from your car – or you won't use it. Meanwhile, you'll be paying for insurance and a parking permit. You'll also have money tied up in the car or in car payments. That money could be going for your education. So, skip the car.

Most colleges have pedestrian campuses. If they're large, there is free or low-cost bus service. Some city bus systems are also free for students. For example, student fees pay for city bus passes at the University of Colorado in Boulder. At the University of North Carolina in Chapel Hill, there is free bus service throughout the whole community. Many buses have bike racks, so students can bike and bus to classes.

Many campuses and surrounding communities have excellent bike trails. Bike racks are often right next to classroom buildings. So, many students commute to class and around campus on bikes.

Some college communities even have loaner bikes for students who can't bring one from home. Iowa City, the home of the University of Iowa, has a community bike library (bikelibrary.org). Local volunteers run it. It even has tools and equipment so students can keep their loaner bikes tuned up.

There is usually bus service from campuses (even in small towns) to other cities. Megabus (megabus.com) has convenient low-cost bus service that includes many college towns in the US and Canada. Passenger trains service many college cities, particularly on the east coast. Many of these, like AMTRAK, have student discounts.

You might need a car occasionally for things like a job interview. If you're 21, you can rent one. Rental companies usually charge extra for people under 25. But if you belong to some groups, such as USAA (an organization for military personnel and their families), rental agencies won't charge extra. Smaller car rental companies sometimes rent to people as young as eighteen.

If you need a car for a job interview, the employer will usually pay for it. Organizations get discounts with car rental companies and have agreements that include younger drivers and insurance. If you have an interview and need a car, ask about the procedure for setting up a rental. If you need a car for a student organization event, your school may have loaner cars available. My son often borrowed a van from his university to drive a group of students to an event.

Some companies, like Zipcar and EnterpriseCarShare, have hourly car rentals on or near campuses. Car share companies usually don't charge extra for younger drivers. However, if you're under 21, you may need your parent's permission to rent.

SUMMARY

Unless you're commuting, you don't need a car for college. You'd have to pay to park it and probably wouldn't use it much. Use public transportation or get a bike (and helmet) instead. Take advantage of the great trails on and around campus. Then rent a car if you need one occasionally.

CHAPTER 36 – FIND LOW-COST ENTERTAINMENT

So, what are you going to do for fun at college? On many college campuses, most classes end on Thursday afternoon. For many students, Thursday, Friday, and Saturday nights are times to party. And Sunday is to sober up. It's no secret – alcohol is a huge problem on college campuses. It's a problem for both underage and legal age drinkers. Drinking is a form of entertainment for too many students. And under the influence of alcohol, people often make very poor choices.

Say "no" to alcohol. Focus on healthier and less expensive entertainment. If you spend money on alcohol, you're (literally) flushing money down the toilet. And fines for underage drinking are high. In most states, you'd pay at least $500, plus court costs. Plus, you'd have legal fees. The costs go up if it's a repeat offense, if you use a fake ID, if you're publicly intoxicated, or if you're driving under the influence. So, think before you drink!

There's so much to do in a college community besides drink. Almost all colleges sponsor free or low-cost movies, readings, dances, and more. Consider volunteering to usher at concerts and plays. You'll see most of the performance – free.

When I was in graduate school, I worked on the first aid team for concerts. We dealt with an occasional drug overdose, someone who'd had too much to drink, or a fainting spell. But we mostly enjoyed the concerts – with great views of the stage.

Students can often get low-cost or free tickets to concerts, symphonies, ballets, and other events. Students in honors programs and student government leaders get these free on many campuses.

Some schools have a student events fund, so lower-income students can get free tickets. Ask at the financial aid office to see if you might be eligible. At other schools, if there are unsold tickets shortly before performances, students get them free. Ask at the box office.

Many schools have recreation programs supported by student fees. Most baccalaureate colleges have free basketball courts, soccer fields, swimming pools, weight rooms, and more. Others, like the Outdoor Programs Office at Warren Wilson College in Asheville, North Carolina, have a lot more. They sponsor regular hiking, mountain biking, and horseback riding trips. They have other trips for canoeing, kayaking, hang-gliding, cross-country skiing, rock climbing, and caving. Check to see what is available at your school.

My teens both took board and card games to college. It seemed a little nerdy at first, but they found friends who were also looking for low-cost entertainment. Most dorms have TVs and DVD players. Board games, DVD and game rentals, microwave popcorn, and a big bottle of soda can provide a lot of cheap entertainment on a Saturday night.

Most dorms don't provide dinner on Sunday evening. My son took advantage of his dorm's kitchen. He cooked inexpensive Sunday night meals for his pals. Beyond low-cost meals, it led to some great friendships and wonderful memories.

SUMMARY

There are many low-cost entertainment options on college campuses. Get free or low-cost tickets to concerts, plays, and other events. Create your own entertainment with board games, rented movies, and inexpensive snacks. Don't let alcohol become your entertainment.

CHAPTER 37 – LOOK GREAT – ON A SHOESTRING

Do you need new clothes for college? My son once knew a young woman who maxed out her student loans. She then went on a clothes-buying binge every time she got her loan disbursement check. How stupid! I'm sure the clothes wore out years before she paid off those student loans.

You don't need many clothes for college. Dorm closets are small. Plus, if you fly to school, you can spend a lot shipping clothes back and forth. So, figure out low-cost ways to look great without spending a lot of money.

When I needed an outfit in college, I always checked to see if my sister had one I could use. She lived nearby and was about my size. I saved by borrowing clothes from her. Many of my friends occasionally borrowed clothes from someone down the hall, especially if it was something they didn't need often, like a party dress.

Many students shop Goodwill, St. Vincent DePaul, Salvation Army, or other resale shops. Our local Goodwill has a quarter day every Wednesday. What a great way to pick up a jacket or coat. One student told me she got a brand new pair of jeans – with the tags still on – for a quarter!

Second-hand stores and consignment shops can also be great sources for clothes when you interview for internships or jobs. You probably need only one or two outfits. Look for washable clothes rather than ones that need dry-cleaned. The costs of professional dry cleaning can put a dent in any budget.

If you decided to get your hair washed, cut, highlighted, and styled, and then got a manicure and pedicure for a big event, you could easily spend several hundred dollars on a single Saturday. But you can look just as good — and pay a lot less. Look around for nearby low-cost hair salons and cosmetology schools. Better yet, find one that also has coupons in the campus paper or online. You want to look your best, but it doesn't have to cost a fortune. If several friends are going together, be strong enough to say, "Sorry, I can't afford it," or, "I've got other priorities for my money." Friends may appreciate your honesty and join you in skipping foolish spending.

I was embarrassed in college. I felt like everyone had more money than I did. But I decided to be honest about it. If people judged me by the labels on my clothes and the amount I spent, they probably weren't great friends anyway. Interestingly, the guy I dated in college (and now my husband) tells me he appreciated my honesty. He didn't have much money, either. So, it was nice to find someone else who was used to living on a tight budget. We had many zero- or low-cost dates, but we had fun. And we both graduated from college without any debt.

SUMMARY

There are many ways to look great in college without a lot of money. You don't need many clothes for college. If you need an outfit for a special event, see if you can borrow it. Or find one at Goodwill or another resale shop. Use low-cost hair salons. You'll want to be look good, but within your budget.

CHAPTER 38 – GET INCOME TAX BREAKS

A re there tax breaks for college? Can you get them? How? There are many income tax breaks for students and families paying for college. There are state and federal tax incentives. This book just covers federal income tax breaks. Check your state department of revenue website to learn about your state's tax incentives for college.

TAX BREAK TERMS

Let's start by reviewing key terms. An incentive is something that motivates you to do something else. The government encourages people to do things by giving them tax breaks. There are two groups of federal tax incentives for higher education. The first group encourages people to *save* for college. The second group encourages people to *go* to college. Chapter 4 covers incentives to save. This chapter covers the others. A tax credit reduces the income tax you pay. A deduction reduces the amount of income taxed. So, a tax credit is worth more than a deduction of the same amount.

AMERICAN OPPORTUNITY CREDIT

Many college students (or parents) qualify for the American Opportunity Credit. It offsets what you pay for the first four years of college by reducing the amount of income tax you (or your parents) pay. It allows you (or parents) to claim up to $2500 per year in college expenses. Expenses can be for tuition, books, or other required materials. You have to enroll at least half time for one term during the year at an eligible school. Almost all accredited postsecondary schools are eligible schools.

This credit phases out at higher income levels. Forty percent of the credit (up to $1000) is **refundable**. This means you can get the money back, even if you don't owe taxes. You have to file a federal income tax return to get the credit, even if you aren't otherwise required to file a return.

LIFETIME LEARNING CREDIT

You can get a Lifetime Learning Credit for years you don't claim the American Opportunity Credit. Generally, you'd use this credit once you've used up your eligibility for the American Opportunity Credit (for example, after four years of college). Higher-income taxpayers don't qualify for Lifetime Learning Credits. Eligible taxpayers can claim either the American Opportunity *or* the Lifetime Learning Credit, but they can't claim *both* for the same student in one year.

For each tax year, you can claim a Lifetime Learning Credit up to $2000 (per return, not per student) for qualified expenses paid for postsecondary education. There's no limit on the number of years you can claim the Lifetime Learning Credit. And you don't have to be aiming for a degree or studying half time to qualify. So, the lifetime learning credit may be very helpful for lower- and middle-income people who take one or two courses at a time over several years.

TAX BREAK RULES

Before you claim college expenses, get up-to-date tax information and read it carefully. You can't use every income tax incentive for the same person at the same time. There are also income limits. The limits are different for each incentive. Each incentive also has specific definitions of eligible expenses.

You also can't claim expenses that you don't pay. For example, if your employer, a scholarship, or a grant covers an expense, you can't claim it on your taxes. If you're a dependent on another person's tax return, only that person can claim these expenses. If you're not a dependent on another person's tax return, only you can claim these expenses.

You can't claim the American Opportunity Credit or Lifetime Learning Credit for education expenses that you pay with money from a tax-advantaged savings plan such as a 529 Qualified Tuition Program or Coverdell Education Savings Account.

If parents pay education expenses for more than one person in the same year, they can choose to take credits on a per-student, per-year basis. For example, they can claim the American Opportunity Credit for you and the Lifetime Learning Credit for your sister in the same year. So, you need to choose among the incentives you claim. Use the Internal Revenue Service (IRS) Interactive Tax Assistant tool (at irs.gov) to help decide if you're eligible.

1098-T

Schools send information about your education expenses to you and to the IRS, using Form 1098-T (called a Tuition Statement). Most students will get a 1098-T form for the previous year by January 31. Not every student will get a one. For example, if waivers, scholarships, or grants cover your tuition and fees, you may not get one. The 1098-T contains information that can help you (and the IRS) figure out if you're eligible to claim education expenses on income taxes.

You may get your 1098-T by mail or electronically. Save it. Then give it to anyone who claims you as a dependent on his or her tax return, if you don't claim yourself. Some schools report only tuition and fees on the 1098-T. If your 1098-T doesn't include amounts you paid for eligible course-related books, supplies, equipment, etc., use your own records to calculate the amounts you paid for these items.

Scholarships and grants are normally not taxed. If you're working toward a degree and you use scholarships and grants to pay for required tuition, fees, books, supplies, and equipment, your scholarship and grant funds don't count as taxable income.

TAX BREAKS FOR STUDENT LOANS

There are also special tax breaks for student loans. Interest (other than for home mortgages and home equity loans) usually isn't deductible on your income tax return. However, there's a special deduction for interest paid on student loans. The deduction, phased out at higher income levels, can reduce your income subject to tax by up to $2500 each year. You can take advantage of this deduction even if you don't itemize. When you complete income tax forms, you can claim a **standard deduction** (a set amount) *or* you can **itemize** (list) specific expenses. You usually can't do both. However, you *can* take student loan interest deductions, even if you claim a standard deduction. Forgivable student loans (see Chapter 29) also get tax breaks. If a student loan is forgiven because you worked for a certain number of years in a specific profession, you usually don't have to pay extra taxes.

GET FREE TAX HELP IF YOU NEED IT

I've never found IRS publications easy to read or understand. But the IRS website (irs.gov) provides details about these tax breaks. The National Association of Student Financial Aid Administrators (NASFAA) also provides information about them. You can find information at nasfaa.org in the section for students and parents. If you're confused, find a free or low-cost service to help you figure out income taxes. For example, accounting students at the University of Northern Iowa (one of the top accounting schools in the country) provide free tax help on campus each year. See if accounting students on your campus provide similar services.

SUMMARY

There are many income tax breaks to help pay for college. Check your state department of revenue website to learn about your state's tax incentives for college. Each incentive has specific rules. So, you need to figure out which incentives you can claim. Use the Internal Revenue Service (IRS) Interactive Tax Assistant tool (at irs.gov) to help decide if you're eligible for federal income tax breaks.

CHAPTER 39 – DON'T WASTE TIME

Don't waste time. That sounds simple, doesn't it? But it's amazing how many students take five or more years to get a four-year degree. In fact, according to Complete College America, it now takes full-time students, on average, 3.8 years to earn an associate degree and 4.7 years to get a bachelor's degree. Most students don't plan to take five or more years to get a degree. So, how does it happen? If you drop a few classes, change majors, and fail a course or two, you can suddenly have another year (or two) to pay for.

There are many incentives to finish bachelor's degrees within four years. One big incentive is that many scholarships and grants only pay for eight semesters. And most financial aid requires students to make "appropriate progress toward the degree."

If you only plan to pay for four years of college, and then take five or six years to finish, you're going to run out of money. Or you're going to go deeply into debt. Even worse, you may drop out before earning your degree. People who drop out before earning their degrees often have serious financial problems. They often have high student loan debt, but they're stuck in low-wage jobs. Those who fail to repay a loan on time are **in default**. According to a 2014 report from the New America Foundation, college dropouts have the highest student loan default rates.

Some schools charge students more for courses beyond requirements for their degree. Remember, to graduate with a given major, you must have specific classes, not just the minimum number of credits. So, if you don't pay close attention to requirements, or if you change majors, you can end up with extra credits, but still need required courses to get your degree.

Other colleges use positive incentives to get students graduated on time. For example, in-state students at many four-year public schools in Texas can earn a $1000 tuition rebate if they complete degrees within three credit hours of the number needed to graduate. The goal is straightforward: "minimizing the number of courses you take – saving money for you, your parents, and the State of Texas."

Take a Full Course Load

Unless you're working full time, take a full course load – at least fifteen credits. The federal government considers you a full-time student if you take at least twelve credits per semester. However, most bachelor's degrees require about 120 credits. Do the math. You can't graduate in four years if you only take twelve credits per semester unless you also go to summer school or earn credit for prior learning. If you're going to graduate in eight semesters, you need to average fifteen credits each semester.

Most colleges charge full tuition for twelve or more credits per semester. And most schools don't charge extra if you take more than twelve. For example, a college might charge the same tuition for eighteen credits. Usually there's a limit to the number you can take at one time (typically eighteen).

If you can do well with a heavy course load, it may even make sense to pay extra to take more classes. If you do, you can reduce the time needed to graduate. For example, if you take one extra three-credit class each semester, you can probably graduate a semester early. That's a semester of tuition, fees, room, and board expenses. And you can get into the job market and start earning a paycheck sooner, too.

CHOOSE CLASSES CAREFULLY

Many students change career plans and majors part way through school. That's the reason that many colleges and universities don't make students declare a major right away. Even if you think you know what you want as your major, focus first on general education classes. Then, if your career interests change, most credits can still apply toward your degree. Also, if you decide to transfer schools (as many students do), general education credits are more likely to transfer than specialized credits.

DEVELOP GOOD STUDY HABITS

Studying in college is different from high school. For example, high school teachers and parents often make sure you go to classes, pay attention, and complete homework assignments. In high school, you spend a lot of time in class and less time studying independently. It's the other way around in college. A college class might only meet a few hours each week, but you might need to read and study another ten or twelve hours independently. Many students find it hard to manage that new independence and responsibility.

Most colleges have classes and services to help you develop good study habits. You'll also find good advice on YouTube (search "college study habits") and on sites like wikihow.com/Develop-Good-Study-Habits-for-College.

DON'T DROP COURSES

Don't get into the bad habit of dropping courses. I had a college friend who dropped classes every time she didn't like the instructor. She even dropped the same anthropology class a couple of times before she realized the professor was the only one who ever taught that course. And she needed it for her major. She finally faced the situation, stuck with the class, and surprised herself by earning an A.

When I teach, I often have students who fall behind or who get a low grade on an exam. They sometimes start down the path toward dropping the class. I always call them in, try to convince them to keep going, and help them get back on track. Dropping courses wastes time and money.

If there's a good reason you've fallen behind, most professors will let you to take an **incomplete**. An incomplete lets you suspend work on the class. You don't get a grade or credit right away. Once you're able, you can complete class requirements at little or no added cost.

FIGURE OUT YOUR MAJOR AND THEN STICK WITH IT

Switching majors can add a year or more to college. So, try to figure out your major and then stick with it. Until you know your major, try to take classes that apply to many majors.

Some schools have career exploration programs during the first year of college. If you don't take a career exploration course, visit the career-planning center – early and often. These centers have many tools to help decide how your interests, values, and skills align with careers. They have details about the job prospects in different fields. And they can help you get internships and a job when you graduate.

If you don't find help at your career services office, look at career planning tools online. For example, the US Department of Labor publishes the *Occupational Outlook Handbook* on the Internet (bls.gov). It's a free, easy-to-use guide with information about hundreds of occupations. It describes what employees do at work, working conditions, the training and education needed, earnings, and future job prospects. Chapter 3 lists other free web-delivered career planning sites you can use.

DON'T SWITCH SCHOOLS

Don't switch schools unless you've planned the transfer. Hundreds of thousands of people have taken a few classes at several colleges. They've spent a lot of time and a lot of money. But they aren't much closer to a degree than when they started.

When you take all classes at one college or university, the classes usually build upon one another. They're like pieces of a puzzle that come together to provide the big picture. You develop a full set of knowledge and skills needed for your career. When you take classes at multiple schools, the classes often don't fit together in an orderly way. You may have overlaps among classes and big gaps where you're lacking important skills and knowledge.

If you expect to move frequently, try to find a school that offers an online degree. You'll get a better education, more quickly and less expensively, than you'll get taking classes at multiple schools.

IF YOU NEED HELP, ASK FOR IT

Make a plan for how you'll get your degree in four years. If there's a suggested course sequence for your major, follow it. Meet with your academic advisor regularly. And stick with the plan.

However, sometimes students get off track through no fault of their own. For example, there may not be enough teachers or spaces for all students who need a course. This is common at public schools in high-population states like California. Your best bet in these cases is to register as early as possible and register for classes held at off-peak times. Early morning, late afternoon (especially Friday), Saturday, and evening classes are more likely to have open slots (or shorter wait lists) than classes at other times.

If you can't get into a class needed for graduation or to stay in a course sequence, go see your advisor right away. And go see the professor teaching the class, too. Many professors will try to add students to a class if they know how much depends on it. If you're wait-listed, try to keep up with the class by watching online lectures and doing reading assignments.

To get around these issues, some colleges (such as University of the Pacific in Stockton, California) offer four-year graduation plans. The student agrees to develop a plan and meet regularly with their advisor. They also agree to register early, apply for financial aid on time, take a full class load, not drop classes, etc. In return, the university pledges to get the student graduated in four years. If you meet the requirements and a course isn't available, the school substitutes another course, waives the requirement, or pays tuition and fees to allow you to take the course later.

If you're struggling in college (for whatever reason), get help! The transition to college is tough. And many of us have learned to hide our problems. In a word – don't!

Many students who've dropped out of college could've made it if they'd gotten help. All colleges have advising, mentoring, tutoring, and mental health services. Don't be too proud, stubborn, or embarrassed to ask for help if you need it. If you don't know where to turn, ask your academic advisor or your resident advisor. Or call student counseling or mental health services. If they don't help, call the dean of students' office and tell the receptionist what's bothering you. These people know where to find the help you need.

SUMMARY

A great way to save money in college is to not waste time. Take a full course load and plan your course of study carefully. Don't drop classes or switch majors without very careful consideration. Don't switch schools unless you've carefully planned your transfer.

If you're struggling in college (for whatever reason), get help!

CHAPTER 40 – TAKE SUMMER CLASSES

What should you do during summer break? You need to make summers count. One way is to take classes.

It may make sense to take college classes the summer after high school graduation. It's a good time to take a remedial class or a study skills class, so you're ready for credit-bearing classes in the fall.

Some schools have extended orientation programs, designed to help students transition to college life. Many target students who are the first in their families to attend college. These programs often include sessions on study skills and financial aid. They also give students a built-in network of friends when classes start in the fall.

You may also want to attend summer school after your first year in college. Students usually can't find good internships after just one year of college. Many lower level (freshman and sophomore) courses are available in summer and classes are often small.

Some accelerated degree programs require summer school. Or you may need summer school classes if you decide to get a double major or some extra credential. For example, I needed one year of summer school to pick up an additional teaching certification.

Summer school can be a real bargain. Many schools offer lower prices in summer. Lower tuition and room rates keep facilities in use year-round. If dorms are too expensive, find an apartment to sublet. Near universities, apartments often have August 1 through July 31 leases. But many students leave during the summer. So, you can often sublet apartments at bargain prices. Another way to save on housing is to work as a resident advisor (RA). Some regular RAs leave in summer. So, universities need people to fill in. RAs get free single rooms and sometimes get free meals or free tuition. Some RAs work in dormitories with adults (for example, teachers taking classes to update skills). Others supervise junior or senior high school students attending academic, music, or sports camps.

Even the most expensive private colleges usually allow students to take summer classes at another school and get transfer credit. So, maybe you can live with a parent and take summer classes at a local college or state school, paying in-state tuition. You can then transfer credits back to the college where you'll complete your degree. If you want to do this, check ahead to make sure credits will transfer.

If you're studying at an in-state school, you might want to broaden your experience by attending summer school somewhere else. For example, at New York University's Summer in New York program visiting students can take classes in art, dance, drama, musical theater, film, television, photography, and more. University of Southern California, which has one of the top film programs in the country, also has a summer program. Summer students have gone on to become producers at major studios, independent filmmakers, and even Emmy Award winners.

Many schools schedule travel and focused, single-topic classes in summer. If your campus doesn't offer these classes, look at other universities with an exchange agreement. Review the ideas in Chapter 13. Consider how you might develop an unforgettable summer experience.

SUMMARY

Summer school classes can be a great way to save money. Or they can be a wonderful way to enrich your college experience. If you decide on summer school, make sure your financial aid will cover it. Some scholarships and grants don't. And, make sure credits will transfer before taking summer courses at a different school.

CHAPTER 41 – GET INTERNSHIPS

What's an internship? Should you consider one?

One of your college goals is to prepare for a satisfying and well-paying career, right? Internships help reach that goal. They provide money for college and help you get a better job when you graduate.

GET ONE OR MORE INTERNSHIPS

Internships are short-term jobs, usually for a summer or a semester. Internships let you try a career or a company without a long-term commitment. Some students find such a great fit, they get jobs at graduation. They may even get a bonus or work credit for the internship.

Students often have two or more internships with different organizations. For example, you might try to have an internship with a for-profit business and another with a non-profit. Or you might have internships in different industries or areas of the country. For example, my nephew planned internships in the three cities where he most wanted to live after graduation.

Almost every school offers internships. Some colleges and many majors *require* internships. Some fields of study use a different name to describe on-the-job experiences. For example, if you're an education major, you'll complete **student teaching**. In social work, you'll probably complete a **practicum**.

The length, structure, and salaries vary by school, field, location, and employer. Students earn income for many, but not all, internships. For example, student teaching and practicum assignments rarely pay. Non-profit internships often do not pay, either. However, your school may have scholarships available to cover your expenses in these programs.

Business and engineering internships at large companies and in major cities pay the most. A few business internships come with extras such as a company car, entertainment, or an expense account. Some, especially in large cities or overseas, provide housing in college dorms or company-owned apartments. However, money and extras aren't the only things to consider in selecting an internship.

Internship experiences vary from clerical assignments to high-level projects. They can be on campus, or they can be in a foreign country. Internships can be as short as one month to as long as a year. Some schools charge no tuition for internships. Others charge full tuition, even though you're not on campus or attending classes. Some are non-credit experiences and others offer credit similar to on-campus classwork.

Some schools set up internships with small companies. Students learn what it's like to manage and grow a small business. I heard about a Midwestern small business owner who used internships to identify people who might be interested in buying his business when he retired. The students gained solid business experience working with him. And he found a young woman to buy and build his business. He sold her the business at a fair price, and even financed it. Plus, he worked with her part time until she was confident running the business alone.

Many schools have programs that teach students how to start businesses. Sometimes these include internships with startup companies. For example, the Mayfield Fellows Program at Stanford University is a nine-month program for engineering students. They learn from startup founders and investors, and work in paid internships.

Occasionally, internships include scholarships. For example, Morgan Stanley (a financial services company) provides a $5000 scholarship for junior and senior years of college with a paid internship the summer between. The program targets minority and **LGBT** (Lesbian, Gay, Bisexual, or Transsexual) students interested in finance.

Begin exploring internship opportunities during your first year of college. Check with your department and the career services office. Professors in your major department may also know about internships.

Sometimes there's a career academy or professional development class offered for your major. If one is available, take it. These can help develop your job search, resume, and interviewing skills. Students in these classes often get top internships.

Read business magazines and newspaper business sections to look for opportunities. You can also find internships online. Visit:

- College.monster.com
- Vault.com
- Internships4you.com

Contact Chambers of Commerce and economic groups in the area where you'd like an internship. And look for internships on websites of federal, state, and city government offices and non-profit groups.

Talk to other students about internships. Attend internship programs and job fairs on campus and in your hometown during breaks. Get information about internships directly from company websites or through their human resources offices.

MAKE THE MOST OF YOUR INTERNSHIPS

Consider internship opportunities like job opportunities. Think about the projects you'd complete. Would they be challenging? Consider your supervisor. Do you think he or she would be a good coach and mentor? Talk with other students who have worked there.

Think about the location. Can you find affordable housing? Is the salary enough for your needs? Also, think about the long term. Would you like a career with this organization? Is it in an area where you'd like to live?

Treat your internship as the first job in your career. Dress appropriately. Sharpen your work habits, arriving on time, working independently, staying on task, and finishing projects on schedule. Work hard to turn the theory you've learned in classes into practical skills. Use the opportunity to understand the organization, competitors, and the industry. Watch and learn from people around you who are good at working in teams, handling problems, and communicating. Ask questions and volunteer to help on extra projects. Figure out if this career is a good fit. Even if you decide an organization isn't one you'd like to join after graduation, good references will help you get another good job.

SUMMARY

Strong internships are great ways to apply classroom learning to on-the-job situations. A well-paying experience can also help pay for college, especially if you can live inexpensively during the internship. These experiences build your resume and usually lead to better job offers when you graduate.

CHAPTER 42 – CREATE AFFORDABLE INTERNATIONAL EXPERIENCES

Would you like to study abroad? Every student can benefit from living and studying in a foreign country.

Only wealthy students used to study abroad. But today it's common for students at all income levels. Students at every type of public and private college can enjoy international experiences. Even community colleges have international programs. And many times there are special grants and scholarships to help pay for these experiences.

Study abroad programs can be as short as two weeks (for example, during a January break) or as long as a year. They can be in English or in the language of the country. They can involve classroom learning, research, service learning, or some combination.

There are many service-learning opportunities for students with healthcare, engineering, and education majors. And some volunteer opportunities have no restrictions about majors. Volunteer projects tend to be shorter-term than other experiences. For example, it's common for January term classes to include international service-learning experiences.

INTERNATIONAL BRANCHES OF US SCHOOLS

There are different ways to get credit for international education. One way is to study at an international branch of a US school. About 100 US colleges and universities have branch campuses in foreign countries.

Some schools have campuses in more than one other country. For example, Temple University, based in Philadelphia, also has campuses in Tokyo, Japan, and Rome,

Italy. US schools have campuses in Canada, England, Greece, Spain, Italy, Japan, Singapore, Qatar, the United Arab Emirates, and more.

AFFILIATE PROGRAMS

You can also study through an affiliate program. In **affiliate programs**, you study at a foreign school associated with a US one.

When colleges have affiliate agreements, you usually pay the US school. The tuition is often the same as you'd pay at the US school. There are sometimes extra administrative fees. Plus, students usually pay travel expenses.

The US school does not have to be where you're getting your degree. It may be less expensive to study through a community college or in-state university. You then transfer credits to the school where you intend to graduate.

DIRECT ENROLLMENT

You can also **direct enroll**. You enroll in the foreign school, pay the school directly, and then transfer credits to your home school. Students who direct enroll sometimes have more options for low-cost airfare and low-cost housing.

My daughter direct enrolled in a German university one summer. She stayed in a youth hostel, shopped in local markets, and rode subways and trains. I used award miles to buy her airline ticket. So, her total cost for the experience was less than she'd have paid for summer classes at her home school. I called her "frugal fräulein" (fräulein is the German word for young woman).

However, when you direct enroll, you don't have much support from the foreign school *or* your home school. And few scholarships or grants pay for direct enrollment. So, it isn't common. The only other people I know who've done direct enrollments had family connections in the foreign country.

IMMERSION PROGRAMS

Immersion programs involve students deeply in the culture and language of another country. You often live with a local family. So, rather than speaking English and talking with other US students at dinner, you're talking with your host family in their language. It's inexpensive compared to staying in hotels, dormitories, or even hostels. Plus, you experience the culture first hand. You eat local foods, enjoy local entertainment, and join in events you might otherwise miss. My daughter once lived with a host family in Spain during Holy Week and Easter. She said it was fascinating to join in Spanish traditions.

You can also immerse yourself in a culture without living with a host family. Students who immerse themselves in a country save money and learn more. For example, local foods cost less than foods imported from the US. You can travel inexpensively using local buses, subways, and trains. This is also a good way to learn a language − in and out of the classroom.

Students who study abroad this way may even learn a new language well enough to earn college credit by exam. (See Chapter 8 for more information.)

LEARN ABOUT INTERNATIONAL EDUCATION THROUGH YOUR SCHOOL

A good starting point to learn about international experiences is your home college website. Look for "study abroad," "international education," or "global learning." Then visit the office in charge. Most colleges and universities are eager to provide global experiences for students. So, many have special scholarships or grants for international study. Many scholarships don't consider financial need, so all students are eligible. Some schools, like the University of Denver with its Cherrington Global Scholars Initiative, charge students nothing extra for international study. The program even pays for international airfare and student visas. Students only pay extra for their personal expenses, like weekend trips in the country.

UNDERSTAND POLICIES

It's easiest to arrange international experiences through the school where you plan to graduate. Your home college helps you enroll and get your student visa, housing, credit transfer, and more. But shop around and compare prices before you decide. First, figure out how to transfer credit to your home school. Then look at websites of other US schools. Check out the sites of community colleges and other schools where you'd get in-state tuition.

Studyabroad.com provides general information about studying abroad, plus information about specific schools. It has a search engine and discussion boards where students can ask questions and share ideas. It also includes some information about scholarships. The Council on International Education Exchange website (ciee.org) covers study abroad opportunities in about forty countries. If you want to explore programs by country, look at studyabroadlinks.com. These sites also have information about study abroad scholarships.

Check to be sure your scholarships and grants will apply if you take part in an international program. Some may have restrictions about international study. Usually, if you enroll at least half time in the foreign school, your federal financial aid (such as a Pell grant) will apply. If you take part in a study abroad program that costs more than your home school, you may even be able to get a larger Pell grant. Visit the study abroad section of the US Department of Education website (studentaid.ed.gov) to learn more.

Talk to your advisor before you make definite plans. Make sure courses will transfer and apply toward your degree. And be sure you know and follow correct procedures. Also, the deadlines for international programs are early. The international program must accept you before you can apply for scholarships, grants, and your student visa. If you study abroad, you may also disrupt course sequences needed for your major. So, think about and plan for international experiences. Allow time, and meet all application deadlines.

INTERNATIONAL INTERNSHIPS

Taking classes, conducting research, and volunteering in a foreign country are all common. International internships are less common. But it may make sense, especially if you want a business or international relations career.

Students who complete international internships must have work visas from the host country. These are more difficult (and take longer) to get than student visas.

There are many ways to find international internships, including through your college internship office. Multinational companies often arrange internships through college placement offices.

Some companies include an international rotation as part of their co-op program. When they do, they often handle travel, housing, work visa, and other arrangements, making it easier for co-op students.

AIESEC promotes international exchange for students and recent college graduates. It's an international, non-profit, student-run, educational foundation. The website (aiesec.org) includes information about internships. Also, check the internship section of the studyabroad.com website.

SUMMARY

International experiences can be some of the most valuable parts of college. Students on budgets shouldn't pass up international experiences without thoroughly exploring possibilities. I didn't think I could afford study abroad in college, so I didn't even look into it. That was a mistake. Give yourself chance to enjoy an experience of a lifetime. International experiences may be a lot more affordable than you first think.

It takes some effort, but you can save thousands of dollars by shopping around for international education experiences. The decision about where to enroll depends on several factors. It depends on your home school's policies on transfer credits, scholarships, and grants. It also depends on monetary exchange rates. Just as you looked at net prices in deciding where to apply to college, look at net prices of study abroad opportunities. Remember, the net price is the amount you pay *after* scholarships and grants.

Think about and plan for international experiences. Wherever you decide to study, make sure you talk to your advisor at your home school before you make plans. Make sure courses will apply toward your degree. And be sure you know and follow correct procedures.

CHAPTER 43 – TRY THESE
COST-SAVING IDEAS

What else can you do to save money in college?

Start by taking a money management class. Many colleges offer classes called Financial Literacy, Personal Finance, Money Management, or something similar. Many schools offer these classes for credit. Some even require them. If your college or financial aid office has one, sign up for it. Some are online, but most have in-person sessions. Go to the in-person sessions. Nothing beats listening to people talk about their problems caused by too much college debt. It'll send chills up your spine when you hear young people talk about having to live with parents for years, postponing marriage, children, and buying a first home. You'll come away with a new appreciation for getting your degree with little debt. You'll make a budget, and stick to it.

Previous chapters all describe tactics that can save a thousand dollars or more. This chapter deals with smaller tips, hints that can save $25, $50, $100, or $200. But as my grandma used to say, "All those nickels add up."

Just as a movie matinee costs less than a Saturday night show, some colleges have lower prices for classes at unpopular times. Many schools also offer reduced rates for summer school for the same reason. **Off-peak pricing** lets colleges more fully use their buildings, and you save. Take advantage of the discount if your school offers it.

Most students head to college with a personal computer. But schools have computer labs with free internet access in class buildings, the library, and dorms. Public libraries have them, too. It's convenient to have your own, but you can save if you use a free computer instead. Plus you won't need to buy insurance for it, either. If you need your own, look into buying hardware and software through your school. Most schools sell them at special low prices. And some non-profit schools don't charge sales tax, either. Also, don't sign up for mobile services you don't need, don't duplicate services, shop for the best rates, and stay within your plan limits.

Look for student coupons and discounts, especially during the first few weeks of classes. Look on bulletin boards and in welcome packages.

Drink tap water. Studies show city tap water is cleaner and purer than bottled water. And it's free! Carry a reusable water bottle and refill it at public fountains and water stations. Then skip soda fountains and pop machines.

Skip expensive coffee shops and make coffee at home or in your dorm. Some college departments and student lounges also have free coffee. Many students spend $10 a day on sodas, coffee, and other drinks. Drink tap water and other free drinks, and you'll save more than $3600 each year.

If you smoke, stop — now! Smoking is a no-win deal. It costs a lot, especially when you consider the cost over many years. The cheapest cigarettes cost about $7 per pack. If you smoke a pack a day, that's more than $2500 each year. If you smoke for ten years, that's $25,000! Smokers also pay higher healthcare, home, and life insurance rates. You might as well be smoking dollar bills! And smokers have lower life expectancies. Also, think about the inconvenience of smoking. You can't smoke on most college campuses. Most restaurants, dormitories, apartments, and workplaces are also smoke-free. And employers may not even hire you if you smoke. So, if you smoke, find a smoking cessation program and quit — now!

SUMMARY

There are many ways to shave college costs. Look for ways to save each day. Think twice before you spend.

CHAPTER 44 –
IF YOU NEED HELP, GET IT!

College isn't easy. There's a lot of pressure. You're figuring out a major and career path that affects your whole life. You're trying to do your best in classes, even if you don't enjoy them. You may be figuring out new relationships. And you probably have to worry about money, too.

You don't have to face these issues alone. Every campus has people to help you. Schools have counselors, with some available 24 hours a day, seven days a week. They can help you work through things that are bothering you.

Pinpoint what's upsetting you. Then search the campus directory to find an office that sounds like it could help. There are offices to help you with learning. There are others to help you with relationships. There are others to help with physical or mental health issues. And there are people who can help you through a financial crisis. You're not alone.

If you can't pinpoint exactly what's bothering you, or if you're not getting help, talk with your resident advisor or call the dean of students' office. If you feel like you're at the end of your rope, call a crisis line or 911 and explain your situation. Remember, there are people who want to help you.

Some of my biggest regrets in life are those times when I didn't know someone needed help. I evidently didn't communicate that I was willing to help. And it didn't seem like they needed it. You'd probably be surprised how many students and professors are willing to provide help if you let them know you need it.

I know several college presidents. Every one of them cares deeply about students at their school. Your president may not know you by name, but I'm sure he or she cares about your well-being. If you've tried the counseling offices you know about, and you don't know where else to turn, call the president's office. The president won't be right there to take your call. But the person who answers the phone will work on his or her behalf – and try to find you the help you need.

Far too many students drop out of school because they don't feel there's any alternative. Don't make a big decision like that, without giving people a chance to help you. If you're considering dropping out, take advantage of the resources around you. Use them to help you reevaluate, regroup, refresh, and refocus your energy.

Some of the most difficult financial situations occur when people have student loan debt, are partway through their degree, and then drop out. Student loan debt is challenging in any situation. But if you have debt without a diploma, you usually can't get a good job to pay off the debt. So, before you drop out, make sure you've gotten help from the people who are there to help you. And if you must quit school, make a plan to **stop out** rather than **drop out**. Start planning your strategy to get back on track to earn your degree.

SUMMARY

Every college has counselors to help students who are experiencing problems. If you need help, get it!

CHAPTER 45 – FINAL WORDS

Thank you for reading this book. I sincerely hope you've learned many ways to save on college costs. I hope you'll get your degree without taking on too much debt.

Not every strategy is right for every student. There is no *right* answer for every student, or even one *right* strategy for any single individual. Every student must figure out the pieces of his or her personal college puzzle.

It's important to develop a plan, and then follow your plan. It isn't easy. And remember, "plan" isn't just a noun. It's also a verb – an action verb. Plans change because you change and circumstances change. Keep this book handy and refer to it often. Reread parts and review your plans, making changes, as needed. In the words of my first boss: "Make a plan, and then work the plan."

You *can* afford college. You can get your degree at an affordable price. You don't need to go deeply in debt. But it isn't simple. With the ideas in this book and a strategic plan, you can save tens of thousands of dollars on college. It's worth investing your time and energy.

Remember Seneca's words: "Luck is what happens when opportunity meets preparation." I hope you're now prepared to take advantage of the wonderful college opportunities ahead.

Good   luck!

NOTES